TO THE UNKNOWN HERO

TO THE
UNKNOWN
HERO

HANS ERICH
NOSSACK

translated from the German
by RALPH MANHEIM

FARRAR, STRAUS AND GIROUX
New York

Library of Congress Cataloging in Publication Data

Nossack, Hans Erich.
   To the unknown hero.
   Translation of Dem unbekannten Sieger.
   I. Title.
PZ4.N87To4   [PT2627.0759]   833'.9'14   73-85729

TO THE UNKNOWN HERO

Precisely.

An old suit is no proof. If you as a lawyer say so, I as a historian have all the more reason to. Especially a suit fifty years old. No, wait a minute. My father must have bought it secondhand. That suit may have been as much as sixty years old. At best I might be able to prove that it was one or two sizes too big for my father, which would tend to—what's your legal term for it? Thank you, that's it—to exonerate me. And thank the Lord the suit has almost certainly ceased to exist in its original form. Old Sophie must have cut it up to make trousers for her grandchildren. You can bank on that.

I've told myself all this a hundred times. And what happens? I go to bed. I'm tired. I've been correcting papers all evening. I've had a hard day and I have to be in school the next morning. I need my sleep. I've always been a sound sleeper—I really have. Never taken sleeping pills or anything of the kind. Not even Sominex. My wife can't get over my insensibility to noise. The poor thing! If somebody on the third floor flushes the toilet, she hears it. Not to mention the planes. And in the morning she's a wreck. I even think it rather annoys her that these things don't bother me. And now what happens?

I go to bed. We've said good night, I've switched off the bedside lamp; as I've told you, I'm dead tired. I usually fall asleep on my right side. I don't know why. It probably has something to do with my heart, though

3

my heart is as fit as a fiddle. An old habit, I suppose; anyway, it's always worked. But now? I'm just dropping off, going under so to speak, you know the feeling, and suddenly something inside me snaps back and I simply can't get to sleep. I lie awake for hours. I sweat and shift from side to side. And I have to pretend to be asleep or my wife will start asking me questions. Even so, she remarks on it in the morning. You had a restless night, she says. Yes, I say, it must be the cheese, I'd better cut out the cheese at dinner. After that, of course, the cheese disappears from the dinner table. As if it had anything to do with cheese! It's the suit. Especially when I'm half asleep and off my guard, that old suit comes dancing in. I see it on its hanger, sliding back and forth on the clothesline; the trouser legs puff up, and the whole suit seems to shake with laughter. After that, there's no hope of sleep.

And then the other day. At last week's symphony concert. You see, we subscribe. We've had the same seats for years. My wife is very fond of music, why not; besides, it's a good thing, you meet all kinds of people. What would become of our town if our kind of people didn't support these things? All right. It's true, we're in deep mourning for my father, but this was a serious concert, I don't see how anyone could object. They played Telemann and naturally Beethoven, and then some Brahms, I think. Forgive me, I don't really remember. My wife always keeps the programs. Oh well, there isn't much else going on here in Celle.

4

Well, they played, they played magnificently. Our local rag said something about a "gripping interpretation." Even the word "revelation" came up. The usual superlatives, what would you expect? But speaking of revelation . . . believe it or not, while they were playing the *Eroica* or Chopin's *Revolutionary Étude* . . . ah, now it comes back to me, there was a young guest pianist, what's his name again, world-famous, one of those Slavic names, and naturally he played Chopin, he would, because remember, Chopin was a Pole. Beg your pardon? Heavens, no! Why should I have anything against the Poles? On the contrary, their tragic history, torn between East and West; how could I as a historian find fault with that? But if you let me finish my story, you'll see what I'm getting at: in this purely private affair of mine an amazing number of Polish names keep cropping up, and that, to put it mildly, I find disconcerting. Even my father's old suit . . . but first let me tell you about the concert.

Well, while this virtuoso is reeling off his arpeggios, I can't help thinking of that old suit, which prevents me from enjoying the music. Of course there's an association. Revolution and *Revolutionary Étude*, and the suit is connected with the revolution, though not the one Chopin had in mind. But doesn't that seem pretty far-fetched? Why should I worry about a suit while I'm listening to a pianist? I even forget to applaud. The people clap like mad and jump up. My wife shouts Bravo! As a rule she's very reserved, but with music

5

she's carried away. She gives me a dirty look because I'm not clapping and haven't stood up. Didn't you like it? Of course I liked it, it's just that I'm so moved. So naturally I jump up and clap until my hands are sore. I wouldn't have wanted to seem ungrateful to the young man who'd been knocking himself out at the piano. On the way out, we meet one of my colleagues and his wife. Wasn't it breathtaking? Shall we have some beer together? So we go to the Deutsches Haus for beer. We talk about music and the topics of the day. A pleasant evening.

Now at least I can talk about it. My wife has taken the children to the Black Forest for a week over Easter. In the car, of course. For three it's cheaper than the train.

But to get back to the suit: I'm no fashion specialist, but to judge by old photographs it seems to have been made about 1910, definitely before the First World War. The trousers, for instance. Rather tight and tapering, they might almost be in style again. Beg your pardon? No, no turn-ups. Precisely! Just like today. My wife felt the material, men don't understand those things. Excellent quality, she says, English, badly worn, but you can still tell. And a waistcoat, that's another significant point. In 1910 a man wasn't properly dressed without a waistcoat. With a buckle at the back. Antediluvian. Amazing the way it's lasted. Two wars, revolutions, inflations, depressions, dictatorships; whole cities have been destroyed, but this suit has survived. Doesn't it give you pause?

What's more, a suit that can't have fitted my father. And another thing: as far as I can remember, he only wore double-breasted suits, and this one was single-breasted. And even supposing he wore single-breasted suits as a young man and only switched to double-breasted later on, because they seemed dressier or more imposing for business purposes, this suit must have bagged at the waist and the trouser legs must have looked like corkscrews. My father was much too neat a man for that kind of thing and my mother would never have let him wear it. All indications are against it. And assuming that the suit was made around 1910, the whole thing becomes positively absurd; because in 1910 my father was only fifteen or sixteen. You see? Why should he have bought a secondhand suit at that age?

My father was a little shorter than I am. I guess I take more after my mother or my grandparents. They were tough, gnarled Heath peasants, a magnificent type. You should have seen my grandmother walking down Lüneburger Strasse. As stately and erect as a queen! You won't find many like her today. My father was tough and wiry too, but shorter, as I've said, and more agile.

My mother keeping the suit all this time—fifty or sixty years—isn't so unusual in itself. An Uelzen woman never throws anything away, even if she hasn't the slightest use for it. You can be sure that she packed it carefully in mothballs and had it hung out on the balcony and beaten at least twice a year. In my mother's lifetime I'm sure it was kept in the moth chest; she wouldn't have had it in the wardrobe with the regular suits; it would only have taken up space. That must be why as a child and as long as I lived at home I never saw the suit or heard of it, though as I know my mother, she must have grumbled quite a bit every time she put it back in the moth chest. For sixty years, mind you.

The first time this silly suit was mentioned in my presence was, wait a second, yes, it was in 1951. Precisely! At a kind of family engagement party in Uelzen; only my parents, my fiancée, and myself. It must have been in the autumn, because the school term started next day and I had to go back to Celle. No, I'm sorry, but in this case the exact date doesn't matter. And of course I didn't take the suit seriously. I simply thought it was an old bone of contention between my parents, something my father made jokes about. I took everything he said and acted out that evening as a joke, his way of making fun of me, my brand-new doctorate, my first teaching job, and academic knowledge in general. My father was brilliant at that kind of thing. He was such an actor that most people didn't even know he was making fun of them. Of course I didn't take it amiss, I was used to it. We laughed ourselves sick. I found it most amusing. Think of it: amusing! When it was the naked truth. The naked historical truth, and I, a trained historian, didn't realize it until twenty years later—yes, that was almost twenty years ago. Amusing, you'll admit.

Of course I can cite certain considerations in my defense, in justification of my blindness, if you want to call it that. Not my engagement, no, I don't believe so. After all, my parents knew my fiancée. Her father was the manager of Praesent Werke, the big flour mills, and everybody knows everybody else in Uelzen. And she had gone to school at the Girls' Gymnasium on Schillerstrasse. No, it's more likely that what blinded me so at the time was my doctor's dissertation, which I had presented two years before at Göttingen University. It was brimful of scholarly apparatus and I was very proud of it. Or, to be more precise, since this was in 1951, what blinded me wasn't the dissertation itself but the popularization that a Düsseldorf publisher had brought out. With my consent, of course. The book was a success. It made money, we may as well be frank, and I was very proud of being able to marry without any help from my father. If you think of it in that light, you can't really find fault with me. After all, what could my father, a successful businessman who had hardly ever been outside of Uelzen, have known about the period I had dealt with in my dissertation? Yes, of course, he was alive at the time, but in Uelzen, far from the events under discussion, whereas I had collected documents for years and subjected them to critical examination. Yes, that's how it was.

All that evening we talked about hardly anything

but my book, much to the annoyance of my mother, who would rather have discussed the forthcoming wedding. Of course, that meant more to her. The book had just come out and I had presented my father with a copy, expecting him to be pleased. I had thought he'd be proud of his son, because my dissertation had been well received and I had my doctorate. Maybe he was proud of me; my mother certainly was. You know how it is. May I ask what your father was? Ah, a notary? That's a different story. It means that academic education was taken for granted in your family. My father had a peasant background, he was self-made. A son with a doctorate must have struck him as a big step forward. But never mind that.

Well, in the course of the conversation about my book, my mother happened to mention this suit. Just one of her usual comments on household affairs, I thought, and attached no importance to it. Besides, I had something else on my mind. My father seemed to doubt the historical accuracy of my book, and frankly that upset me at first. It disturbed me that this conversation should be taking place in the presence of my wife, that is, my fiancée; I didn't know how she'd take it. Afterwards I explained that this was my father's way, she mustn't forget that he was a shopkeeper; he developed this manner in dealing with his customers from the country. His little jokes and winks made a big hit with them.

Actually it wasn't so much a conversation as a one-man performance. As I've told you, my father was a born actor. Naturally he kept lapsing into Platt-deutsch, and he didn't bother much about grammar. Altogether, he loved to bamboozle people. It made my mother very cross. I myself as a child felt ashamed now and then when my father played the clown. It was my mother, by the way, who called it that. God forbid that I should call my poor father a clown. One of the city's most progressive businessmen, that's what it said in his obituary. Yes, Uelzen can be proud of him.

Well, my mother mentioned the suit in her grumpy way, as though speaking of one of her life's aggrava-tions. And after her death, when my father broke up housekeeping and moved into the two rooms on the second floor where he died . . . no, I beg your pardon, he died in the hospital. There's an anecdote about that too; at least I hope it's only an anecdote, invented by one of the night nurses or somebody. We won't go into it now, it's too exasperating . . . Well, after my mother's death my father must have taken the suit out of the moth chest and hung it up in his wardrobe. This was confirmed by old Sophie, who kept house for my father and took care of his clothes. Actually she's not so old, she's still living in my grandfather's old house in Johnsburg, the house where my father was born. A whole street of small, very old houses, all the same. It still has an open fireplace, and behind it there's a narrow strip of vegetable garden that reaches down to the Ilmenau. Very romantic for us children; but now, with the new city planning, all that will go. My grandparents kept the old house even after the business expanded. This Sophie's mother had gone to work for my grandmother. She was Polish. There used to be a lot of Polish women in the town—before my time, that is. They worked at the Uelzen sugar mill. Today they'd be called seasonal workers, but a lot of them stayed on and married. The only thing I remember about those women is the kerchiefs they wore on their heads, that's how you could recognize them. Anyway, this Sophie told us the suit had always been hanging there, that was all she knew about it. And after my mother's death, there was plenty of room in the wardrobe. An enormous old wooden wardrobe; my wife and I are still wondering if we can find room for it in our house. As for the moth chest, my father gave it to us right away. It's in our attic, my wife keeps our winter clothes in it. A good solid chest, some kind of exotic wood.

But why did my father feel the need of keeping this suit after my mother's death? That's the question that puzzles me. What's that? A psychological problem? You can't be serious. Can you do anything with psychology in your office? There, you see. Neither can I as a historian.

All right. The suit is no proof either, not even the label. I mean the silk label that tailors sew on suits, usually on the coat collar and more recently on one of the inside pockets. What does it amount to? An advertisement. An advertisement is no proof. I'm pretty sure that any judge would laugh you out of court.

This label was sewed to the coat collar. The first thing I did was to cut it out with my penknife. Not to destroy a proof, because it's not a proof, but ... well, I just did it spontaneously.

My wife, of course, was surprised. "Don't cut holes in the material," she said and gave me a suspicious look. That was the day after my father's funeral. A big funeral! Most gratifying! The mayor said a few words over his grave. With this man a phase of our city's history has passed away. That's what the mayor said, and it's true. I was glad, partly because of my wife, to see my father had been duly honored. Afterwards there was a gathering at the Hotel Stadt Hamburg. As it happened, we were staying there. There was no point in shuttling back and forth between Celle and Uelzen. We wouldn't have been comfortable at my father's place or with my wife's relatives. Besides, you know relatives.

Well, next day we looked through my father's things to see what we could use and what should be given away. That kind of thing takes a woman's eye. Old Sophie was there helping us. Every item that was taken out of the cupboards and chests of drawers made her cry. Really touching. Yes, it was sad work. There wasn't much we could take. Some bed linen, a few kitchen towels, and such things that any household can use. But the suits, good Lord! They were in first-rate condition, but to alter them would have cost more than they were worth. My father had sold the business soon after my mother's death. For a very good price, you can bank on that. In such things he was an old fox. The store was the most modern in Uelzen, self-service and all, not to mention the fine location on Lüneburger Strasse at the main intersection. One of those companies with stores all over the place snapped it up. My father invested the money in gilt-edged securities. The company kept the name of Kurt Hinrichs over the door, it still lights up at night. They thought it was a good idea because of the customers from the country.

So there we were in my father's bedroom, emptying the wardrobe. We make two piles; one for what we can use and one for everything else, that is, what we were leaving for old Sophie. After all she had taken care of my father all through his last years. Even when he died unexpectedly in the hospital, she was the only one there. I mention that because I wouldn't want you to get any wrong ideas about me. I talked it over very thoroughly with old Dr. Schleppegrell, who's been our family physician as long as anybody can remember; I think he even brought me into the world. He lived a few doors down the street. It was old Schleppegrell who had insisted on moving my father to the hospital after his first dizzy spell—yes, it happened in his room, and luckily old Sophie was with him at the time. They phoned me to say there was nothing to worry about, a mere precaution. Otherwise I'd have run right over from Celle, it's no distance at all. Yes, most distressing, but it can't be helped now. Old Schleppegrell said that in such a case a reliable diagnosis was impossible, that with his constitution my father might just as well have lived to be a hundred. Just to be on the safe side I asked old Dr. Link, the pharmacist—you know how doctors are always at daggers drawn—and he said the same thing. Besides, as I gathered from a remark that Dr. Schleppegrell let fall, my father seems to have forbidden him to worry the children for nothing. That would have been just like him; he didn't like to take help from anyone. Well, there you have it, and it was old Sophie who closed his eyes. Naturally she cried at the sight of every single thing we left her. All the china, incidentally, because it wouldn't have gone with a modern apartment. We took only a few pieces that have become antiques by now, things that came down from my grandmother's family. An old clock, for instance; it must be quite valuable. It's hard for me to get used to hearing it strike in our apartment. Especially at night.

Well, as the suits were taken out of the wardrobe, they were thrown on the bed. That was when this old suit turned up. I almost didn't notice it, because my wife and Sophie were just getting ready to throw another on top of it. Believe me, I'd have been much better off. Old Sophie would have taken the lot and made them over for her children and grandchildren, or sold them to a peddler for all I care, and I'd never have wasted a thought on it.

But, unluckily for me, I notice the label and it gives me pause. No wonder. Because what does it say?

HUBERT JAWORSKY. Yes, another Polish name, or maybe Czech. I'm haunted by Polish names. But the name alone wouldn't have disturbed me. Why shouldn't there have been a Jaworsky in Uelzen before my time? I've already told you that there used to be a lot of Poles working at the sugar mill. So why not a Polish tailor? No, it wasn't the name but what was under it. What do I see? CUSTOM TAILOR and under that, framed in a complicated old-fashioned curlicue: RATHENOW. That damned curlicue pursues me in my dreams.

Rathenow, I ask you. Have you ever been in Rathenow? Neither have I, and I have no intention of going there. But the point is: what has my father got to do with Rathenow? I ask you. And I asked myself then. As far as I know, he was never in Rathenow. What would he have been doing there, in Rathenow of all places? He didn't like to travel. On Sunday we went hiking on the Heath, and that's all. In the summer holidays my mother had to take me to the beach at Timmendorfer, all by herself. Every year there was a big discussion about it. My father always claimed that he couldn't leave the store.

Rathenow. That hit me like an electric shock. Luckily the two women were much too busy with the other things to notice anything and I managed in the nick of time to prevent them from seeing the label. The questions would have killed me. As likely as not my wife would have told one of my colleagues' wives—in all innocence, mind you—that one suit in that pile evidently came from Rathenow. Rathenow would have rung a bell with her because of my book. I leave you to imagine the consequences. It would have been the end of me.

Well, I go through the pockets, I thought I might find something else. I'd done the same with all the suits. But they're empty, only a little bag of moth flakes in the left side pocket and another in one of the trouser pockets. Nothing more, not so much as a crumb of tobacco. Old Sophie took good care of my father. Anyway, he smoked cigars.

Beg your pardon? Why Rathenow? How stupid of me, I was assuming you'd read my book. Author's vanity, especially absurd in the present case. Well, if you had read my book, you'd know that this preposterous city of Rathenow plays a crucial role in it. I suppose I should have gone there while I was working on my dissertation. You might even call it slipshod scholarship. But I believe I can justify myself. Of course, if I'd known about this Hubert Jaworsky at the time, it would have been my duty to investigate on the spot and find out where that suit came from. In the name of historical accuracy, if only to eliminate unwarranted suppositions. But at the time I knew nothing about the suit or Jaworsky; I certainly had no idea that my father had owned a suit made in Rathenow and for some strange reason kept it. On the other hand, to be perfectly precise, this fact would have proved nothing even if it had been known to me. My father could have bought the suit somewhere else, in Hamburg for instance, as indeed he claimed. A label means nothing. Secondhand suits are without history, as it were, though of course a historian can be expected to investigate everything conscientiously.

Since I don't want to bore you with my book, let me recapitulate very briefly; otherwise you won't understand the weird situation I was in. From a historian's point of view, it is beyond question that the military phase of the 1919 uprising came to an end in Rathenow, because it was there that the reactionary or "white" troops, as they were then called, gave up the struggle and dispersed just in time to avoid being encircled. Furthermore, the man who was demonstrably responsible for the conception and execution of the strategic plan that was to culminate in this encirclement—of this there can be no doubt, we have ample testimony and documents to prove it—was last seen in Rathenow, after which he seems to have vanished from the face of the earth. Those are the hard historical facts. That this happened in Rathenow is pure chance. It might just as well have been any other hole between Magdeburg and Berlin.

But please bear in mind that my dissertation had an entirely different title. *To the Unknown Hero*, as the popularization a year and a half later was called, didn't originate with me but with the publisher. Well yes, it is rather flamboyant and I could have protested. Precisely! But in a purely historical sense there was no falsification of the text. Of course I made sure of that. And why should I have objected to their livening it up with contemporary photographs? My word, the book was a success; it advanced my career and made me financially independent. I was in my early thirties and I wanted to get married. But that title! That was what my father made the most fun of. Just wait.

For all its crudeness, the title is historically justifiable. Soon after the disorders a granite block was set up in Rathenow, bearing a bronze tablet on it with the inscription: TO THE UNKNOWN HERO. A photograph of this memorial was reproduced in the popularization; in fact the designer used it for the jacket. Naturally the Nazis removed the tablet in 1933. In the preceding years they had kept daubing it with swastikas. That's another chapter of history. After 1945, of course, the idea of re-establishing the facts that the Nazis had falsified for propaganda purposes, of examining them with scientific precision, was in the air. That's why I selected the topic. And I believe I can say that my treatment of it does not lack precision. Just take a look at the notes, index, and bibliography. The material wasn't easy to come by in the first postwar years, you can take my word for that. I went so far as to admit quite frankly that no certainty was possible concerning that last telegram, which the unknown hero allegedly sent the revolutionary committee in Rathenow from Uelzen—yes, from Uelzen, which gives us a totally unexplained link between Uelzen and Rathenow from the very start. The telegram may be authentic, that is, it may really have been written and sent by the unknown hero. But it can equally well be a forgery, a deliberate deception designed to conceal a political murder. Nothing is definitely established except that it was sent from Uelzen, and the date; the telegram form has been preserved, but nothing can be deduced from it. The message is written in block letters and signed "Hein." The sender's address marked on it is false: a non-existent street in Bardowick. The woman at the post office, a substitute as it happened, was reprimanded for not noticing it. But how could she have been expected to know whether or not there was such a street in Bardowick? They even accused the poor thing of being in connivance with the unknown sender. She suffered a nervous collapse and left the service. If I'm not mistaken, she sued them for damages later on. The woman is still living in Uelzen. I went to see her in connection with my dissertation, but, believe me, I got a very bad reception. Even in her old age she was furious about the way she had been treated. All she said was, "Don't bother me with your stupid revolution!" Then she slammed the door in my face. She was perfectly innocent. You couldn't even call it negligence.

Uncertainty about the authenticity of the telegram fostered all sorts of legends, as uncertainty always does. A historian can't be too much on his guard against that kind of thing. Today it is generally assumed in academic circles that the telegram from Uelzen was a forgery.

They continue to hope that the unknown hero's body will be unearthed in the woods near Rathenow or fished out of one of the lakes. Now and then we hear rumors that the tablet in Rathenow is going to be restored, but so far nothing has come of it.

Yes, generally assumed, and up to my father's death I joined in the assumption. And now? Don't you see what a fix I'm in? I, "Professor Precise," as several generations of students have nicknamed me, have been instrumental in promoting legends, the worst crime a historian can commit! Ought I to return my doctorate? What's that? Ha ha! Precisely. You're perfectly right. It would look like self-criticism in the style of the Marxist deviationists at the show trials. The self-criticism of a paranoiac. After all, I have a wife and children, let's not forget that. Am I to wreck their lives by discrediting myself? Because that's just what I'd be doing, though this time with the truth. The word makes you laugh. I know, all lawyers are cynics. Who was that illustrious colleague of yours who said, "The purpose of laws is to make the truth bearable"? Well said! One thing is certain, that no one would believe my truth. How can you prove it? they'd say. With an old suit and a tailor's label? And where *are* these magnificent pieces of evidence? Don't be ridiculous. Acute megalomania—that's what they'd call it if I were to drag my good old father out of his grave and try to pass him off as the unknown hero. Another difficulty is that the revolutionary movements of the years follow-

ing the first war are regarded as irrelevant nowadays;
at the moment people are more interested in the historical background of National Socialism; unfortunately,
historians also have their fashions.

Am I then to reconcile myself to being the only man
alive who knows the truth but cannot reveal it because
it would ruin me? *To the Unknown Hero*, hm. How my
father laughed when I gave him the book. I can still
hear him. He leafed through it and laughed to himself.
Not loud, but it shook him. I thought he was laughing
at the silly title and felt it necessary to apologize for it.
How can a hero be unknown? he asked. Then he looked
at the pictures. Yes, I remember his taking his glasses
out of his pocket and looking at the pictures in spite of
his laughter. My wife, who was then my fiancée, asked
me afterwards why he had laughed like that. She felt
offended for me. I explained that he regarded scientific
investigation as abstract nonsense that brought in no
money, or something of the sort. I really believed that
at the time, which is why I didn't take his laughter
amiss. It's only now that it all comes clear to me. It's
as if that damned suit, I beg your pardon, were hanging
there shaking with laughter. After a while my father
put the book down on the table and said, "All right,
my boy, let's drink to the unknown hero and your success and your bride-to-be. Mother, come here."

That was in 1951, eighteen years ago. My dissertation,
of course, had an entirely different title: "On the Strategic Genius of the Common Soldier in Revolutionary

Movements, with Special Attention to the German Uprisings between 1918 and 1923." Kind of ponderous, but typical of a doctor's dissertation. Of course, I'd sent my father a copy of that too, but I don't believe he read it; the scholarly apparatus must have put him off. But the subject, as I've told you, was in the air after 1945. It was felt that the Nazi falsifications of history called for rectification. What are you laughing at? Rectification? No need to apologize. A fine rectification! Precisely. The only valid rectification is my father's laughter. Better than a whole bibliography of irrefutable biographical material. On the strength of that rectification—if only they'd heard it—our younger historians could do a little more rectifying.

But don't get my father wrong. As I've told you, he came of a long line of Heath peasants. They're a tight-lipped lot, shrewd and distrustful. Sometimes they pretend to be hard of hearing just to gain time. The other fellow repeats himself, often as not in a way that shows what he's up to. After a while he decides that he's wasting his breath on a hopeless simpleton. Then suddenly our peasant speaks up and closes the deal to his own advantage. The victim doesn't even realize that he's been hoodwinked. Little jokes to take the victim's mind off the subject are part of the same method. And laughter.

I'm only telling you this to show you my father in his true light. By those methods he got to be one of Uelzen's leading citizens. And hoodwinked me too.

But he didn't always laugh. From what I've heard, he didn't laugh when he was dying in the hospital. I've already intimated that there's an annoying bit of gossip about that. Sentimental old wives' tales, if you ask me. My whole being rejects that story. I was going to ask old Dr. Schleppegrell for an explanation. In addition to being our family physician, he regularly drank beer with my father. At least I thought he could tell me whether the story those two women told me piping hot could be true. But then I dropped the idea; the best way to squelch distasteful gossip is to pretend you're not interested. That spoils their fun.

Judge for yourself. My father is in the hospital. No fault to find with the care. Yes, the doctors under-estimated the danger of thrombosis, but you can hardly blame them; such things happen. From what they told us, at any rate, we in Celle were convinced there was nothing to worry about. My grandfather lived to be eighty-six and his father, I believe, to be even older. With never a serious illness. If anything ailed them, they doctored themselves with hot grog and that was that. Tough as the heather on the Heath.

All right. My father's lying peacefully in bed. The nurse, a young thing, brings in old Sophie. She went to the hospital several times a day to see how my father was doing and keep him company. And then she'd write us about it, as we had asked her to do. In her own spelling. Which is worth seeing. Maybe I'll show you one of her letters someday.

On this occasion the nurse bends down over the bed to see whether everything was all right and whether my father wanted anything. He had a private room. Despite the shortage of hospital beds, there had been no difficulty in getting him one. As I've said, he was well cared for.

And then this woman, the nurse I mean, sees that my father is crying. So she claims at least. Big tears flowing down his cheeks. Sophie was standing behind her, and both of them spread the story. Isn't it dis . . . ? But wait. The best is still to come.

The nurse asks, "Are you in pain, Herr Hinrichs? Should I call the doctor?" And while she's wiping away the tears, or so the story goes, my father answers—I'll quote verbatim, because the worst of it is that the wording is perfectly plausible; it sounds almost too much like him—"I'm just giving it a try, child. I never had time before."

Relata refero. Too bad the doctor or some sensible person couldn't have been there to rectify this idle chatter. I don't mean to say anything against old Sophie; she was so weepy herself that she saw tears everywhere, but a trained nurse could have no such excuse. And I'm certain both these women thought they were doing me a kindness and had no suspicion of how their story would make me feel. When my wife heard it, she burst into tears. Then of course she started to reproach me. "I kept telling you to run over to Uelzen." Or something of the sort. Anyway, that was the gist. Suddenly I was to blame for everything. Once a legend gets properly started, it sooner or later comes to be taken for the truth. It doesn't fit my father's character. Take my word for it, he was the last man in the world to blame other people for his troubles. He didn't make things so easy for himself. Now and then even he got swindled: rubber checks and that sort of thing; he'd only shrug his shoulders and say, "A sharp bastard!" With a note of admiration, in fact. And as far as he was concerned, that was the end of it. Yes, that was how he was; I ought to know him, it seems to me.

But enough about this nonsense. Forgive me for even mentioning it. Let's get back to the suit. Where was I? The label. Precisely. My shock over this Rathenow with the curlicue probably made me clairvoyant. In a flash I saw it all, I mean the situation eighteen years ago when I gave my father the book. With a dedication of course. Did I tell you that? "To my dear father, in heartfelt gratitude." It was meant sincerely, because he had let me go on with my studies, though he would certainly rather have had me take over the business. I hoped he would regard my doctorate as a kind of compensation, that's how I meant it. And that's what I thought he meant when he read the dedication and took the book into the dining room to show it to my mother, who was out there with my wife, clearing the table. "Mother," he said, "take a look at this. 'To the unknown hero in heartfelt gratitude.'" One of his usual jokes, I thought; maybe his way of hiding his emotion. My mother didn't take it seriously either; her fingers were greasy from clearing the table and she couldn't have taken the book even if she'd wanted to. My guess is that when they were back in the kitchen she said to my fiancée, He's a big joker, but don't let him fool you; he doesn't mean it. As for me, I hadn't the slightest ground for suspicion. Neither then nor later when we were comfortably drinking our wine. A very good Bordeaux, a dusty old bottle. My father was a connoisseur; an Uelzen man knows his red wine. My father claimed to have saved the bottle especially for this occasion, to drink to the unknown hero in style, as he put it. I thought he was referring to me with my brand-new doctorate and my engagement. How was I to suspect that he was making fun of me and my book and himself? Or even later, when he criticized the book in his comical way and acted out his conception of the events and what he would have done if he had been the unknown hero. I was only amazed at his imagination, because his version fitted in perfectly with the historical facts, which must have been totally unknown to him. I had too high an opinion of my book. But what a piece of acting! I wish I could make you see it. And how we all laughed! My father, who was fifty-five or fifty-six at the time, ran around as if he was on a stage. My mother was thoroughly exasperated. She kept pleading with him, "Father, sit down, for goodness' sake. You're making us nervous." My father would sit down for a few minutes, but then he'd jump up again with my book and start gesticulating.

It wasn't until I saw the damned Rathenow label that all this took on a new significance for me. Clairvoyant or not, I had presence of mind enough to realize instantly that this Rathenow had to disappear. And that wasn't all I realized. I said to myself that if I only removed the label from this one suit it would attract notice and I'd be hearing questions till my dying day. Something had to be done. I toss the suit back on the bed, pick up one of the others that was already lying there, and start cutting out the labels; naturally they were all from Uelzen. My wife is right beside me. What's the sense in that? she asks. And old Sophie, standing there with an armful of clothes, looks at me goggle-eyed, probably for fear that I was cutting up the suits that had been left to her. To my wife I merely said, I'd better cut them out; there might be talk if I don't. That was just the right thing to say. My wife saw the point. It's strange how you often get the right idea at moments like that. She only cautioned me not to make holes in the material, and Sophie asked if she should get a pair of scissors and help. Just get on with your work, I said; the thread is so rotten I can manage without scissors. When I had finished, I gave Sophie all the other labels to throw in the garbage; I had put the Rathenow label in my pocket when no one was looking. Later on I threw it in the toilet at the Hotel Stadt Hamburg and flushed it down. The danger was averted.

28

Any papers, you ask? No, nothing of any importance. You can imagine that I went through my father's desk . . . a big old mahogany thing, incidentally; the moving men got into quite a sweat carrying it up our stairs. An antique. My wife thought there must be a secret drawer in it, and actually there was, though not so very secret . . . Anyway, I went through the desk and all the other drawers and shelves very carefully, but except for neat bundles of receipts from the last few years and similar papers that an orderly businessman is obliged to keep, I didn't find the slightest scrap. Nothing personal at any rate. It must have been my father's habit to tear up all papers of a personal nature. Yes, a very good idea. And as for his will, that must interest you as a lawyer, everything in it was so perfectly clear that any dispute would hardly have been possible. That must be quite unusual. A small annuity for Sophie and a few trifling bequests. Apart from that he naturally left everything to me. Almost all in fixed-interest securities deposited with the Uelzen Savings Bank. No real estate; I believe he got rid of it all in the last years of his life; maybe he thought it was simpler. He had even sold the old house in Johnsburg, the one in which he was born, probably because those decrepit old houses cost more in upkeep than they bring in, and besides they'll all be condemned by the new city plan.

We acquired a small car. My wife had always wanted one, for carting the children around and for Sunday outings. Well, why not? Once we had the car, of course, we started going to Uelzen fairly often. Hard to avoid. One of my wife's sisters married in Edinburgh, can you imagine? To a young Germanist at the university there; that is, he was young at the time. He was teaching at the Uelzen Gymnasium—one of those exchange programs. She was teaching there too; that's how they met.

I'd prefer to steer clear of Uelzen, but what can I do? My wife shows the children all the places she had childhood memories of, her school on Schillerstrasse, the old railway underpass between the sugar mill and the city park, and of course the Ilmenau and the bridge—the girls used to throw their balls in, and then they'd run around the island with their hair flying in the wind and fish the balls out of the water at the next bridge. She keeps asking me, Do you remember? Of course I remember. And to keep up the tradition, we have lunch at the Hotel Stadt Hamburg. One of the waiters is as old as the hills and knows me or claims to. Otherwise I hardly see anyone. I do my best to avoid meetings with old school friends.

Even so, I get a queasy feeling whenever I have to cross Lüneburger Strasse or eat lunch at the Hotel Stadt Hamburg. Go ahead and laugh. You see, my father was one of the town notables. There's a round table there at the hotel where they used to meet. It had a special little flag on it that I remember admiring as a boy. Well, the little flag is still there. So I'm sitting there with my family, choking on my food. My wife

30

sees that something is wrong. What's the matter? she asks. Isn't it good? It's marvelous, I say. Give me some more of the red cabbage. It's a dream. Like my mother's. There, I had gone too far; that could have been taken as disparagement of my wife's cooking. Anyway, the damned red cabbage had nothing to do with it. My trouble is the secret that my father managed to keep all his life and that I have to keep now. I don't even dare to look at that round table in the dark corner, for fear of giving myself away. I feel as if my father were sitting behind my back, quietly smoking his cigar. And suddenly he asks in a voice so loud that everybody can hear, my family, the waiter, and the other guests, Why isn't the unknown hero enjoying his food? It would have been just like my father. Usually he preferred to listen, but now and then it amused him to throw you off with one of his little remarks, though his tone was always so amiable that no one felt offended.

Well, I struggle through the proceedings, that is, the meal. By then I'm in such a hurry to get out of Uelzen that I suggest taking our coffee in Ebstorf. But it can't be done. We have to visit old Sophie first. My wife has a present for her, of course, and Sophie regularly bursts into tears. Those are my Sunday outings. Well, I shouldn't complain; it doesn't happen every Sunday.

At first, in the weeks just after my father's death, I even had to put up with reproaches from my wife whenever she saw I was depressed. You just have to get over it, she said. Your father lived a full life and he didn't suffer long. Think of what my poor father went through. Fact. Her father had cancer of the stomach. All in all, though, it was better having her think me depressed than absent. That was what I was trying to hide. Even during my classes I caught myself drifting off. I don't know whether my graduating class noticed it; those rascals notice everything and interpret it in their own way. In the middle of the lesson I see my father standing at the door of the classroom; he's chewing his cigar and grinning. Once or twice I actually caught myself sniffing the air for cigar smoke. My students probably thought I had a cold, and to be on the safe side I blew my nose. It was bad, though; I'm only beginning to get over it now. After all, I'm not a neurotic. It was . . . how can I make you see it? Imagine you're sitting in your office with a client who wants you to draw up a contract or a will. And all of a sudden the thought hits you: what's the use of all this nonsense— begging your pardon—all these stipulations and safeguard clauses. There's bound to be a quarrel no matter what you put in. Are you going to tell your client that? Certainly not. Instead, you throw in one more safeguard clause and your client goes home happy; you'll get your fee and the world will keep going around very nicely. Quarrels? You won't give them a thought. Why should you? You see what I mean? What business is it of anyone else's what you think? What business is it of anyone's that I accidentally hit on the truth? The truth is neither a legal nor a historical fact but a private affair. It's only private affairs that stir up quarrels. Don't you agree? Only the truth leads to quarrels. So we'd better keep it to ourselves.

It goes without saying that in my classes I now avoid the years covered by my dissertation; if I didn't I might stumble and give myself away. There are plenty of other topics in modern history. As a matter of fact, they're all pretty ticklish. The children's fathers claim that we teach them lies. Fortunately, there are figures and statistics that can't be questioned, or else we teachers would have lost our jobs long ago. And if we stick to figures, the years immediately following 1918, which are my special field, become exceedingly simple. But I don't want to bore you with my professional troubles. Excuse the digression. You were asking me about my father and that evening twenty years ago when he told us the truth.

If I had only inherited just a little of my father's narrative gift! Without it the whole story sounds so colorless and it seems so utterly incredible that we didn't notice anything at the time. We just enjoyed ourselves. And how we laughed! As I was taking my fiancée home, she said, What a wonderful man your father is! And such a sense of humor! Which meant roughly: how can such a successful businessman talk such nonsense? Or the other way around: how can anyone who carries on like that be a successful business-man? You see, before we were married, my wife was secretary to Herr Nahnsen, the wine wholesaler. A thorough gentleman. He supplied the landowners of the region with Bordeaux and Burgundy. A very different clientele from my father's. His wife was said to drink, but that was a long time ago, I was still a child.

And there's another reason why it's difficult to give you a halfway faithful picture of that evening. The story ought to be told in Plattdeutsch. Suppose I were to write a historical work in Plattdeutsch. *Dat is nu all lang her, wol twe dusend Johr*, and so on. Nobody would take it seriously. Even if I wrote about Auschwitz, no one would be horrified. It's more or less as if you were to write a contract or a will in Plattdeutsch. How friendly everything would be at the reading of the will, no quarrels at all.

Naturally my father kept lapsing into Plattdeutsch in making fun of my book. Even the title! How different it sounds, how unheroic as it were. Plattdeutsch was my father's mother tongue. Of course he spoke High German, very correctly in fact when he had to, just as many people speak a foreign language more correctly than their own. But in the store Platt was spoken almost exclusively, because of the peasant clientele and because it's so much simpler to do business in Platt. With my mother too he spoke mostly Platt, though I think she disapproved at first, because her father was a school-teacher in Oldenstadt. After a while, it seems, she gave up trying to convert my father to High German; and then in the store she couldn't help speaking a good deal of Plattdeutsch herself. With me it's different, and with my wife even more so. Among the girls in her gymnasium it was considered vulgar to speak Platt. She still avoids it and sometimes she even pretends not to understand. But of course we can speak it and we certainly understand it. As children we almost always spoke Platt with the other children; anything else would have been unthinkable when we played together or went on hikes. To Unterlüss, for instance, to pick cranberries, that was a kind of tradition. But as I've said, I'm no longer used to speaking it; I got out of the habit at the university and in my work. My wife doesn't like it when I talk Platt to the children. It's bad for my authority, she says, and she's probably right.

At just that time, as it happened, my father was mulling over an important business decision. Quite contrary to his habit, he mentioned it to me and asked for my opinion, though I understood nothing of such matters. Maybe he wanted to play me off against my mother, who was very much opposed to his new plans. All that evening when he wasn't talking about my book, he was talking about his plans. He kept jumping back and forth between the unknown hero and these plans of his. It made us pretty nervous. My mother protested, Father, why can't you sit down? You're so fidgety. As I see it today, my book may have contributed to my father's decision. I mean that my book and my engagement finally convinced him that I couldn't be expected to take over the business. That must have been one of his reasons for deciding to restructure the store along impersonal lines, as they say nowadays. Undoubtedly a hard and perhaps even painful decision for him to make.

His plan, you see, was to convert to self-service. Remember, this was Uelzen in 1951, when self-service stores were unheard-of except in a few big cities. A new departure and a risky one. It could certainly have been a failure. And the risk wasn't only financial. The plans drawn up by an industrial designer at the Braunschweig engineering school must have cost a pretty penny. But as I say, the risk was more than financial. My father had plenty of money in the bank and I'm sure that ample credit was available. But his standing in the business community, his whole existence, was at stake.

A self-service store in Uelzen! With wire baskets on little carts that the customers could push through the aisles, so they didn't have to carry anything. My mother warned him against these wire baskets. She said the women would snag their stockings on them. All the different articles would be displayed on the shelves— the prices of course would be marked—and the customers would roll their baskets along the aisles and take what they wanted. Those labyrinthine aisles. My mother didn't use that word, but she was sure they'd never be able to find anything. But Mother, my father explained, that's the trick of it. That way they see other things, things they'd never thought of, and throw them into their baskets. You see how modern my father's thinking was. And at the end of the labyrinth a cash register that totes up all the items in the basket and spits out the change. There again my mother objected. She had always been in charge of the cash drawer and taken money over the counter. People would get suspicious, she said, when they were given the slip with the total. By that time they'd have forgotten the prices of the various articles and would simply be horrified at having to pay so much. They'd think they were being cheated or that the machine had counted wrong. My father tried to reassure her. We'll give them rebate stamps, at about three percent, we'll work out the right amount, and a booklet to paste them in. Take my word for it, no woman here in Uelzen will let her booklet lapse. They'll keep coming till it's full and they can cash it in; that means plenty of purchases. And they'll keep the rebate for themselves, their husbands won't have to know about it. And another thing, Mother. You won't be able to stand behind that counter forever; think of your swollen legs. And look at what the man has drawn over here, this little glass box, just up the stairs at the back of the store. It's your private office. You'll be able to sit there in comfort and keep an eye on the whole store, every aisle and corner, to keep the employees on their toes and see that there's not too much stealing. Because of course there'll be stealing, the temptation is too great, but we can keep it down and allow for it in our calculations. Well, what do you say?—My mother was never convinced, but she was sick of arguing. Do what you like, you two always know better. With that she closed the debate. Then she went off to the kitchen and clattered about with the dishes.

Would the rural clientele accept the novelty? That was the risk my father was taking. On market days the peasants poured into town from all directions, from Bienenbüttel and Medingen and Ebstorf and Holthusen and Lehmke and Oetzen, and even from farther away. Kurt Hinrichs's store was a kind of meeting place; my father knew them all by name and discussed their affairs with them, just as my grandfather had done when it was only a small shop. That was the only way to do business. You must have seen such shops in small country seats; in those days people took their time. And the same with my mother—that was what she was used to. Come to think of it, my father first fell in love with her in that shop. They teased her about it for years. One morning she comes in and my grandfather asks her, in Plattdeutsch of course, "Well, lass, what'll it be today?" And the teacher's daughter answered him, "A pinch of salt, if you don't mind, Herr Hinrichs." Oho! The story is that my father, who was busy somewhere in the back of the shop where it was dark, heard her snippy answer and said to himself, That's the girl for me. Anyway, that was the story told in the family, and whenever my mother was cantankerous, my father called her a "pinch of salt." I believe he said it again that evening when he heard her clattering around in the kitchen.

It seemed perfectly possible that the country people would be intimidated by a modern store with a neon sign and all the fancy trimmings. But my father was a step ahead of his times, in Uelzen at any rate. He had long realized that the time was past when a shopkeeper could afford to spend half an hour discussing children, health, the weather, and the harvest over every package of cloves. Since the First World War the shop had been enlarged several times. Larger showcases, and so on. Yes, I can remember when I was still a child my father bought up the dusty old dry-goods store next door and broke down the intervening wall. But all that was patch-work. This was radical modernization.

This was the problem my father had on his mind, probably, I tend to think, a good deal more than my book. For him the book that lay on the table beside his plans was only a kind of diversion. Maybe he wasn't too happy about being a step in advance of his times. I'm not referring to the old wives' tale in the hospital; such sentimentalities won't get us anywhere. I'm only trying to put myself in my father's skin. Maybe it annoyed him that I should be wasting my time on the past while he thought only of the future. And worse, on a past which he knew very well but for one reason or another never spoke of. I've already told you there was a picture of the old memorial tablet in Rathenow on the book jacket. My father looked at the picture and then tossed the book on the table with a laugh. "What kind of a hero is that?" he cried. "How can a hero be unknown?"

We were sitting in the good room. It was seldom used. Only on Christmas and such occasions. As a boy I wasn't allowed into it; if I went, there was trouble. And since my childhood nothing in it had changed. The furniture was still in the same places, as though nothing had been moved in half a century despite the thorough housecleanings twice a year. Only the old crocheted cover that was always on the oval table, with fringes hanging down to the floor, had been removed and lay folded over the back of a chair. My mother briskly took it away when we came out of the dining room and apologized to my fiancée with a contemptuous look at the oval table. For those days it was a large apartment. I can't show it to you because the company that bought the store after my mother's death converted the second floor to offices. Anyway, I don't think it would be a very good place to live in these days, what with the traffic noise at the intersection.

We'd eaten in the dining room, which was in the rear of the house and rather dark. The meal had passed peacefully. Naturally there was duck with red cabbage, and for dessert lemon pudding with whipped cream. My mother was a first-rate cook. My father never talked much at meals. He concentrated on his food; eating was an important business and talk was out of place. But of course my mother talked to me and my fiancée about our impending wedding and the household furnishings and other feminine matters. And of course she kept asking us if we didn't like it and why we didn't take more. Any guest of my mother's was stuffed to the gills.

It was only in honor of my fiancée and the occasion that we sat in the good room afterwards. Not at the oval table, good Lord, no. That wouldn't have been possible. The table was an old-fashioned monstrosity. Mahogany of course. One of those things with only one leg in the middle. No, not a leg, it was more like a tree trunk with elaborate carvings and brass casters. An extension table. Actually the extra leaves had been put in that evening. Normally that happened only at Christmas, because of the presents. The leaves were kept in the attic all year long; my father must have brought them down for his own purposes. Because the plans for the new store were spread out on the table, along with the pencils and note pads, on which my father jotted down all sorts of figures.

That in itself made my mother irritable, because she wasn't allowed to touch anything, which meant that she couldn't dust. As far as she was concerned, it was all childish nonsense and certainly had no place in the good room. Apparently my father had forbidden her to move anything; maybe he'd thrown in a word about all the money the plans had cost. And there was something else on the table: my book, *To the Unknown Hero*, which I had given my father before dinner.

"*Ik wil di mol wat seggen, min Jung,*" said my father in the doorway, as he was coming out of the kitchen, where he had uncorked the wine bottle. That was how it started. Then of course my mother brought in mats for the bottle and the glasses for fear of spots on the polished tables. "Let me tell you something, my boy. It's all very well about your revolution, and your writing a whole book about it. It's a great honor. Am I right, Mother? Don't be offended with your old father; I don't know as much about it as you, but I've been giving it thought, you can ask your mother, and it seems to me that you've given it a lot too much thought."

Yes, that's how it started. It started as a joke. But those words were revealing; they showed that my father already knew my book backward and forward. I had supposed that I was giving him his first copy, and before dinner he had shown no indication to the contrary; he had read only what I had written on the fly leaf and thanked me. Actually he had been in possession of the book for a week or two and had read it. His copy was locked up in his desk, perhaps to spare me a disappointment. I still have no idea how he came by it. In those days new books didn't find their way to Uelzen very quickly, the townspeople aren't exactly wild about literature; at least they weren't then. Possibly the publisher in Düsseldorf had taken it on himself to send my father an advance copy because of the printed dedication: "To my dear father in gratitude . . ." Or someone at the notables' table had heard of the book and brought it up in the conversation and my father had sent for it. But that doesn't matter now.

I could infer from my mother's more or less acid remarks that he had read it very carefully. You've been driving him crazy with your book, she said. She herself had picked it up; maybe she had glanced at the illustrations, but that was about all, I think; she didn't have much time for reading. It was enough for her that my father seemed pleased with the book. You can't tear him away from it, she told us; sometimes he really scares me. There I'm sitting with my sewing, thinking about all the things I have to do next day, and all of a sudden he bangs the book down on his knee. What's the matter, Father? You mustn't frighten a body like that. And he says, Goodness, Mother, it's amazing what the boy has thought up. He even runs after me in the kitchen and shows me something in the book. And even in bed he grunts and laughs over it until I'm perfectly furious. That's enough now, Father, I tell him, tomorrow's another day. Yes, that's how it affects him. Though tickled by her complaints, my father justified himself. Seeing it's dedicated to me, the least I can do is read it carefully. My father was anything but a reader. During my childhood there were few books in the house. A Wilhelm Busch album and the Bible of course and a big atlas; I don't even think we had Goethe until I was given a set as a confirmation present. Of course I was proud of my father's interest in my book. I'm not trying to defend myself, but that must have been one of the reasons for my obtuseness. I felt sure, you see, that my father couldn't have known a thing about the period covered in my book, so naturally I assumed that all the knowledge he now displayed came from reading it.

Even so, I was pretty thick. For instance, when after pouring the wine my father suddenly planted himself in front of me and asked, "So the fellow's name was Hein?"

I had gone into the question of his name very thoroughly in my dissertation and satisfied myself that in the newspapers and leaflets that appeared during the two weeks of the uprising he was spoken of chiefly, almost exclusively in fact, as Hein or Comrade Hein. I had not found it possible to determine whether this was a first or a last name. Or it could have been a party name that he had taken during the period of illegality and then adopted officially at the start of the revolution. In two or three articles, which can be disregarded for purposes of scholarship, the name had been corrupted into Heiner; this can probably be explained on the basis of the local dialect. Because of the general strike relatively few papers appeared at the time; they were badly printed, which is also true of the leaflets. The material available to the historian is very meager; the Nazis removed most of it from the libraries and destroyed it.

"He was also referred to as Kuddel," I said to my

father, "but only in two otherwise unimportant newspaper articles."

"What's that? Kuddel? Why, that's my own name. What do you think of that, Mother?"

"Anyway, this Kuddel or Kurt is quite incredible. It must be an auditory mistake."

"Auditory mistake? What's that?"

"It could have been like this. Maybe one day in the excitement somebody shouted, 'Kuddel,' and the reporter mistook it for his right name. Of course I investigated in Hamburg; but either the people are dead or because of the altered situation they don't talk. No, we can safely assume that this Kuddel doesn't mean a thing. In my opinion, it is amply demonstrated that the person under consideration was called Hein and also called himself Hein. Which can also be inferred from the last document, the telegram from Uelzen."

"Anyone can call himself Hein, my boy. I can give you at least twenty Heins here in Uelzen alone. What do you say, Mother? But not one of them is a . . . what do you call it again? . . . a strategic genius. All plain ordinary people like me."

Do you understand? Of course you understand. But I didn't understand a thing, though the naked truth lay on the table in front of me and I had only to reach out for it. My father had shoved my nose in it. His name was Kurt Hinrichs. There you have the Kuddel and you have the Hein. But even if I had noticed the similarity of names at the time, I'd have taken it as a coincidence. The name isn't exactly unusual; there must be other Kurt Hinrichs in the world. It's my son's name, for instance. No, the identity of names proves nothing.

But my father gave me still plainer hints. There he stands with the open book in his hand and points at the first picture. A rare item. There are only two authentic photographs of this Hein, both taken from daily papers of the time and both very indistinct. Except for the printed name below them, they would be without historical value. The first was taken in Hamburg after the storming of the Rathaus, that is, on the first day of the uprising; and the second about eight or ten days later near Wittenberge, in the course of the so-called diversionary march on Magdeburg. The second picture shows even less than the first. This Hein is standing with a lot of other weird-looking figures in the back of a truck with a big red flag. That is, the flag must have been red. He's wearing a long military overcoat that hangs down to his feet, and all you can make out in the shadow of his vizor cap is an unshaven face. When my father showed her the picture, my mother said, "Gracious, he looks like a perfect pig." My father came to his defense. "But, Mother, if the man was a strategic genius, how would he find time to shave?" All this, you mustn't forget, in Plattdeutsch. Nothing sounds very serious in Platt.

There wasn't much to be seen in the first photograph either. A small group of men in front of a field gun, and behind them the façade of the Hamburg Rathaus.

46

"What?" my father asked, pointing to the picture, "you tell me this little runt took the Rathaus? You'll never get me to believe that. Who's the big man next to him? He looks more like it to me. Look at that mountain, Mother. Built like a wardrobe trunk."

"That's Klaus Hundewatt," I told my father.

"Hundewatt?"

"Yes, it's a funny name, but common. He was a long-shoreman. The Nazis killed him in 1933, while questioning him in the Hohe Bleichen. He was a member of the Red Front Fighters."

"What a shame!" said my mother. "Such an imposing man!"

"Why didn't *he* take the Rathaus?" my father asked.

"Because he didn't know how to handle a gun. Th little fellow was in the field artillery."

"Him in the field artillery? No, my boy, you can't tell me that. They take only big bruisers in the field artillery."

"Why, you were in the field artillery yourself," my mother put in.

"With me it was different. They took me because I came from Uelzen; that made them think I'd know how to handle horses. Which I did. And, man alive, it was back-breaking. But that little fellow, no, he'd never have stood it. No one can tell me different."

"He fought in the First World War. From beginning to end."

47

"Him? Don't let them tell you fairy tales, my boy."

"Yes, Father, all the witnesses agree that he did. And since he knew how to handle a gun, no one ever doubted it. It seems just about certain that he had had his training at the Bahrenfeld army post."

"You don't say so! If he'd been in the same regiment, I'd have known him. Because in Bahrenfeld . . . Good Lord, the way they drove me over Luruper Feld, I can still feel it in my bones. No, I never met anybody like that. You should have asked me before."

"He could have been in a different age class. His age has never been determined with certainty. In the testimony it fluctuates between twenty-five and thirty. After his inexplicable disappearance, of course, inquiries were made in the various artillery regiments. But the rosters were all gone. And how can you expect to find a man who goes by the name of Hein?"

"And this sorry specimen is supposed to have taken a whole Rathaus?"

"At least it was taken thanks to his initiative or his ability to handle a gun. That has been definitely established; it's an accredited fact."

"Well, in that case, he was right to disappear. If he hadn't, they'd probably have killed him like the big fellow. Besides, he'd damaged the building. Mother, look at the little runt."

My mother didn't want to look at him. "What's the sense in all this? It will only bore Olga." Olga is my wife. Naturally she said it interested her very much. And finally, because I had written the book, my mother had to put on her glasses.

What a challenge on my father's part to make my mother examine the picture! As if he had actually wanted us to recognize him. Or was he trying to mislead us by pointing so directly at the truth?

Because the best is yet to come. My mother put on her glasses—a long-drawn-out procedure, because as usual it took her quite a while to find them. Then, after examining it rather peevishly for a while, she said, "If he weren't wearing a helmet, I'd say it was you."

I guess I forgot to mention that this Hein in the picture was wearing a helmet that was much too big for him. It looked as though somebody had put an enormous cooking pot on his head as a joke, though the group in the picture was in no joking mood. The helmet covered half his face and its shadow obscured the rest. The features were barely discernible.

But you should have seen my father. He took up a stance in front of us, my fiancée and me, with one foot forward and his right hand in the opening of his waistcoat. "D'you hear what Mother says? A regular Napoleon."

It seemed so comical that naturally we all burst out laughing.

"I only mean," my mother excused herself, "because of his size and his way of standing . . . well, maybe he's a little shorter . . . but also because of the suit. Yes, I remember now, you had a suit just like that in those days."

My father took the book out of her hand. "Suit? Let's see. What about the suit? It's obviously ready-made. You can buy a suit like that anywhere, here in Uelzen on Bahnhofstrasse, or in Hamburg on Mönckebergstrasse. No, a scholar like your boy wouldn't waste his time on that. It shows the styles have changed, and that's about all."

But my mother went right on, "I was only telling the children how you left home in your good blue suit because of the fancy businessmen in Hamburg you were supposed to visit, and just think, when it's all over, your father comes home in an entirely different suit that doesn't even fit him. It's in the chest up in the attic. All the same we were mighty glad when he finally turned up. We were beginning to think they'd shot him dead. We didn't really know what was going on, the paper didn't say much, only that there was shooting in Hamburg. You can imagine how worried we were. Two weeks without news of him. Except at the beginning, a postcard with a view of the Alster and some swans. I can still tell you what he wrote, it could have been yesterday: 'Dear heart'— yes, in those days I was still your dear heart—'I'll be back the moment the strike is over. Nothing to worry about. Your loving Kurt.' I showed your grandfather the card. He examines it, he turns it over and over, and finally he says, 'You can't lose a bad penny.' I was expecting. And in Hamburg they were shooting the whole time."

"Well, Mother, it looks as if they missed me."

"And what do you think? One fine day my Kurt is at the door. We hardly know him in this suit, and he's wearing army boots with hobnails. Grandma screams at him, 'Don't you dare come into my house with those boots, you'll ruin my parquet floors.' We gave the boots away to Konrad the coachman. No sensible man has any use for such clodhoppers."

"It was only for your sake, Mother. If they hadn't stopped their strike, I'd have had to hike from Hamburg to Uelzen. I couldn't have done it in my party shoes. So you see, my boy, I traded them for army boots, just to be home in time for your birth."

Then of course we all laughed again. The idea of my father hiking to Uelzen in heavy army boots to get there in time for my birth! In point of time it wasn't really so urgent, I wasn't born until several months after the disorders. And then the thing about the parquet floors. My mother was every bit as fussy as my grandmother. I've told you how distinguished my grandmother looked, strolling along in her big shawl on Lüneburger Strasse, always so perfectly erect. She was kind of befuddled toward the end, that happens. She talked to herself. It rather frightened me as a child. I'm sorry, I didn't mean to talk about my grandmother. Or about the parquet floors that were always being rubbed to a high polish. In those days they didn't use shellac. But enough of that. What was I talking about? The old suit. Precisely!

Of course there had been some talk about this old suit

in my childhood. And, more important, about my father being in Hamburg during the disorders and coming home two weeks late. You might reasonably say that before writing a dissertation about the events in Hamburg I might have questioned my father as an eye-witness. I tell myself the same thing. But in my defense it might perhaps be said that no one took this Hamburg escapade of my father's seriously; an amusing family legend that was occasionally brought up in company, a kind of youthful peccadillo. My father's friends teased him about it. "Well, Kurt, it looks like you had a narrow squeak." And the women said, "You can't pull the wool over our eyes. I bet there was a girl at the bottom of it." My father seemed to relish this suspicion. He'd pose as a gay Lothario: "If only I could remember her name. I wonder what's become of the poor thing." And the ladies would reply, "Don't worry, she's doing very nicely without you. A yokel from Uelzen was all she needed." And once my mother added, "It looks to me as if she burned your suit because you couldn't stop pawing her while she was trying to iron it." More laughter. And usually my father joined in. Now you see why I couldn't take the episode seriously.

And as far as the suit is concerned, there was such a reasonable explanation that no one thought of doubting it. It's true that my father left for Hamburg the day before the disorders broke out. His father, my grand-father, sent him to introduce himself to the Hamburg firms, as his successor, so to speak, and the future owner of the shop. My father wasn't so very young at the time; he had four years of world war behind him and he hadn't been home long. That may have been why my grandfather wanted to give him responsibilities, to tie him down as it were. Actually my father had married soon after coming home from the army, so there wasn't much to be feared. The Hamburg firms in question seem to have been importers of tropical fruit. Bananas and oranges, and in the Christmas season dates and figs. Maybe sardines and that kind of thing. I don't know much about it. We got our coffee from Bremen, that I happen to know.

It was supposed to be a quiet business trip, but then they started shooting in Hamburg. That was something no one could have foreseen. My father had hardly arrived and gone to his hotel—a small hotel near the Central Station where my grandfather also stopped—when the shooting started. And naturally the firms he was supposed to call on were closed, because the employees couldn't go to work. And no doubt the high-and-mighty gentlemen, the royal merchants, preferred to stay at home for fear of being shot. And because of the general strike my father couldn't even return home. What was he to do? He didn't know anyone else in Hamburg. Well, we now know what he did. That is, I know, because he told us in the minutest detail, except that we thought he was making it up. The version we had heard in connection with the suit sounded much more plausible.

He had got a big grease spot on his own suit, the good blue one he had worn when he left home, axle grease, he told us, and allegedly he had torn one trouser leg. "Imagine the to-do if I had turned up in Uelzen in that suit! I couldn't have faced it. And besides, it was all wrinkled. I slept in it for two weeks, on benches and on straw in empty freight cars. How could I call on those millionaires in such a suit? So I just went to a second-hand clothing store and exchanged it; I only had to pay a few marks extra."

When asked how he got axle grease on his suit, he had a very simple explanation. It sounded so perfectly natural that nobody gave it a thought. Even my mother, who was suspicious by nature, never really doubted his story. When you come right down to it, he didn't actually lie. The axle grease, for instance. I'm sure it was true that he'd got axle grease on his suit, only not in the way we thought. And probably just as true that he'd torn his trouser leg and that the suit was wrinkled because he had slept in it. The freight cars were real, and even the secondhand clothes dealer, except that his shop was in Rathenow and not in Hamburg. But since no one questioned him, my father had no need to invent anything. He simply told the truth and we misunderstood it. That wasn't his fault.

What we understood was this: because of the shooting, and because he didn't know how long it would go on, my father had moved out of the hotel the very next morning to save money. He'd have to account to

Grandfather for his expenses, and probably Grandfather hadn't given him too much to begin with. Enough
for his hotel room and his food and a few pfennigs for
emergencies, but no more. In those days people reck-
oned those things very closely, and it wouldn't do to
give a young man silly ideas. Wait till you've earned
your own money was their motto.

Here I am talking about axle grease. A grease spot.
And I don't even know how big the spot was. It must
have been pretty big and visible if my father thought
it necessary to get rid of the suit. Only for me it wasn't
visible. I, a historian, trained at the university not to
lose myself in speculations but to stick to documented
facts, failed to see the one historical fact, and, what's
more, a fact that was right under my nose. I didn't see
that axle grease. I regarded the spot as a private joke;
to recognize it as the truth would have been beneath
my academic dignity. No wonder my father made fun
of me. And, come to think of it, how do I know that
the tears my father allegedly shed in the hospital—
quite aside from any womanish sentimentality—weren't
another historical fact? Since I wasn't there, he couldn't
make fun of me—that's certainly what he would have
done in his last moments—so instead of laughing he cried.

But never mind that. If I had the courage, I'd write
a historical study with a title . . . precisely! Many
thanks . . . yes, I'd call it "Axle Grease." A title fraught
with symbolism. A twofold symbolism. In the first
place, axle grease for the cart of history to prevent it

from squeaking too much when it rolls through the universities and high schools in the years to come. But more significantly, because this book would show how historical events can be inferred from the trivia of private life. Of course it would ruin me, because a historian with a sense of humor is unheard-of.

So there's my father in Hamburg when the shooting starts. He's just as economy-minded as his father. He takes his things and moves out of the hotel. Sleeping on benches or in freight cars was no great hardship to him; it hadn't been so long since the war, and at the front he had slept under worse conditions. When we asked him if you were allowed to sleep in waiting rooms or freight cars, he explained that everything was allowed in those days because the police weren't functioning. You could do what you liked. And besides, the freight cars weren't being used during the strike. Possibly my father even enjoyed this state of affairs; he certainly liked it better than dressing up to call on the directors of those big firms. But never mind about that.

As for that damned axle grease—yes, I'm sorry, I have to come back to it—my father had a perfectly simple explanation. "I was helping these men who were loading something into a car, perishable goods, I think. Remember, I had nothing to do but wait for this stupid shooting to be over, so I helped them. In those days nobody found it unusual for people to help each other because all order had broken down. They were good fellows, they even wanted to pay me, but I wouldn't let them. Buy me a bowl of soup, I told them, and call it quits. I guess I wasn't very careful; anyway, my trousers caught on a nail. And then I must have collided with one of the wheels while lifting a crate. They tried to remove the spot with gasoline, and one of them wanted to take me home with him so his wife could clean my suit. Yes, they were mighty good fellows, but I don't think even a professional dry cleaner could have taken that spot out."

If I were a detective, I would have asked, Was it really axle grease? Mightn't it have been blood? It seems that bloodstains can't be completely removed, even with chemicals, and certainly not with soap and water. Not my father's blood, because he himself wasn't wounded; if he had been, he could hardly have kept it a secret. But the place was full of dead and wounded who had to be carried away, and my father, who, as he himself said, had nothing else to do, may have helped. But why think up new complications? Let's stick to axle grease. Axle grease is perfectly plausible. The best way to understand what happened is to concentrate on one of my father's remarks: "I had nothing else to do, so I helped them. In those days nobody found it unusual for people to help each other." At the time none of us attached any importance to this remark. But it throws a bright light on the events and on my father's behavior. What's more, it's the pure truth. An astonishing remark. It came back to me after my father's death, when we found the suit from Rathenow, and it's been with me ever since. Look at it from the standpoint of your profession. Suppose a situation arises in which—God forbid—your legal code with all its paragraphs and clauses that ordinarily govern people's lives becomes inapplicable, null and void. What will people do? Because there's nothing else to do, they'll simply help each other, and no one will find it unusual. You think they'd eat each other up? Naturally, you lawyers have always been cynics. My father, in any case, helped; you can be sure of that. It's a historical fact that he helped. Regardless of whom he helped, he helped because he had nothing else to do. You may not approve, but that's what he did.

But whom did he help? That brings us back to our story, I mean, the story he told us when we were celebrating our engagement, and told us with such precision that I, Professor Precise, thought he was only trying to make us laugh. A few weeks ago, to check on my memory, I asked my wife very casually if she remembered that little party at our house and what my father had told us. It was so gay, she said, I'll never forget it! In other words, she'd forgotten everything except our engagement. So much the better, why shouldn't she forget? And if my mother were still alive and I were to ask her, I'm pretty sure she would say, Wasn't that the time he was thinking about converting the store and those stupid plans were lying all over the table and you couldn't even put a glass down for fear of making a spot on the precious things?

True, my father talked as much that evening about the plans as about my book. Every few minutes he'd go to the table and look at them. My mother was exasperated; "Father, forget about those silly plans. That's not what the young people have come for." But my father couldn't be pried away from them.

"What do you say, Mother? What color should we take for the neon sign?"

"Just so you don't make it red!" said my mother. "Imagine your name in red!"

"No, red is no good," my father admitted. "When the people come driving down Gudesstrasse from Hammersteinplatz, they'd think it was a first-aid station. How about white? No, white looks like a funeral. Maybe light blue. What do you think?" And actually the name of Kurt Hinrichs was put up later on in light blue, along the whole housefront. And it's still light blue, as you'll see if you pass through Uelzen.

There were many of these interruptions, during which my father put down the book. But then he'd pick it up again, and sometimes he even held it under my nose.

Let me tell you something, my boy: it's all very well and good the way you explain all that with your scientific methods and documents, as you call them. It's very interesting. A plain man like me can't find any fault with that, I wouldn't dare. And it must have been hard work. But I don't know anything about scientific methods and neither do the people who buy your book. That's why it's all so exciting; I've read it at least three times, from cover to cover. Mother will tell you, she couldn't pry me away from it. Am I right, Mother? And of course it's a great honor for us that you've written such a book, and if you write more of these scientific books, I'll read them all, even if I don't understand anything about science. But what makes this book so exciting is that there's no way of checking up on what you say. Only a man who had lived through it could do that. As it is, we just have to take your word for it, and that's what makes it so exciting. Really, Mother, you ought to read it. You can't keep telling people you haven't had time. What does that make you look like? Besides, it's not fair to the boy after he's worked so hard. Take that ridiculous telegram from Uelzen that the book ends with. It's such a surprise. Anybody who never heard of it because he wasn't alive at the time will be amazed. On that point I can even contribute a little something. If you'd asked me beforehand, you could have thrown it in as a little sidelight, though it's not scientific of course. It was about two or three weeks after your revolution, I don't remember exactly, but anyway things were more or less back to normal. Mother was expecting and wasn't in the store. So one day about noon three gentlemen came in. Well, one of them wasn't a gentleman, that was Police Sergeant Fröhlich. Another was from Town Hall; what was his name again? My poor memory! The third was from out of town, and maybe he really was a gentleman. What brings you here? my father asks them. Old Kastorf, the shoemaker with the basement shop around the corner on Achterstrasse was in the store. Yes, he was still alive then; he always came in at noon to have his bottle filled with schnapps, because then his wife was busy in the kitchen and didn't see him leaving—she was a rough customer. His name was Hein too, come to think of it. Shoemaker Hein, they called him. It's not an unusual name; anyway, he had nothing to do with your Hein, nobody would have suspected him. He was much older and drunk most of the time. One day his old woman comes running in. She hadn't even got through the door when she started screaming, Don't give Hein any more schnapps, you're killing him and it interferes with his work. She had her nerve with her. We couldn't forbid her old man to drink, it wasn't our lookout, and besides we were in business. Well, while these three gentlemen were speaking to my father, I happened to be in the store filling old Hein's bottle out of the big demijohn. In those days it was pretty dark at the back. Naturally I listened with half an ear to what they're saying up front. It was some kind of investigating commission, or whatever they call it. They were investigating in Uelzen on account of that ridiculous telegram, to see if your Hein had any connection with Uelzen, if he lived here, and so on. They got some reception from my father. He had quite a temper—didn't he, Mother? You must remember—and it made him especially mad when officials came around asking questions. Otherwise he was as good as gold. Well, in the course of their investigation they'd found out that I had been in Hamburg during the shooting. We hadn't made a secret of it. What for? We talked about it with the customers. They wanted to know all about it and whether what it said in the papers was true, because there hadn't been any shooting in Uelzen. I suppose the man from Town Hall wanted to make himself important. He had passed the information on to the gentleman from out of town as a great discovery. It had struck the gentleman from out of town as suspicious, and now they wanted to know why I'd been in Hamburg so long. You should have heard my father. He was roaring, 'So here you are! I knew you'd turn up sooner or later. As soon as you stopped your fool strike, and it was high time, the boy came home safe and sound, heaven be praised. Did you expect him to come home on foot because you'd stopped the trains? Is that the new regulation from Town Hall? Step up, son, show yourself to the gentlemen. Let them see that you're yourself and not somebody else! So I stepped up in my long gray apron, with the big demijohn in one hand and a funnel in the other. 'Well, is it him or isn't it? His wife and his mother recognized him right off, you can put that in your report, you can't fool a woman in these things. So what is all this nonsense? Maybe you government people have nothing better to do, but an old businessman has no time for such foolishness. I'm not worried about the boy, he's right here; what I want to know is who's going to pay me damages. Nice of you gentlemen to

62

honor me with your visit, because this way we can settle the matter right now. Twelve cases of oranges went bad on me because of your general strike. When the train finally pulled in, the car stank like a pest-house; I almost passed out. I should have had a gas mask. I didn't even take the stuff, I gave the bill of lading to some people in Veersen, they thought they'd use the rotten oranges in their kitchen gardens, for fertilizer. Go out to Veersen and see for yourselves. The whole place stinks. And what does the insurance company say? The insurance company says they don't have to pay because it's an act of God. Well, no insurance company is going to swindle old man Hinrichs, and no act of God either. No, gentlemen, you've come to the wrong address. I didn't ask for your general strike, anyone in Uelzen can tell you that. The government's going to pay me damages for my oranges or I'll know the reason why. You'll be hearing from me at the Town Hall.' My father could have gone on browbeating those gentlemen for hours, but then we were distracted by a sound behind us— glug-glug. What do you think it was? Old Kastorf was taking a good big swig from his bottle, he couldn't wait any longer. 'Take it easy, Hein,' says my father, 'or you won't have any left for tonight.' We all laughed. The man from Town Hall—what was his name? Mother, wasn't it the fellow that married Grete Hieschen?— anyway, he wasn't very happy about the business with the oranges; nothing but trouble could come of it.

So he apologizes: 'No hard feelings, Herr Hinrichs. Of course we all know you and your son. We're only doing our duty in coming here—just a matter of routine.' 'All right,' says my father, 'let's have a little drink to routine. I've got a bottle right here.' No, they said, that wouldn't do, they were on duty. And then they left. My father looked after them, shaking his head: 'And that's what we pay taxes for.' They never bothered us with their foolishness after that. And in the end the insurance company paid for the oranges, at least in part; my father was a good customer, so they decided to stretch a point. But naturally we didn't give a damn about that.—Well, my boy, it wouldn't have hurt you to put that little story in your book; it's the kind of thing people like to read. An incident like that in the author's own family would have made the whole story more exciting. In that case he must be telling the truth —that's what people would have thought."

Beg your pardon? Did my grandfather know, or even suspect, that his son had taken part in the revolution? No, I don't believe so. From what I know of my grandfather, I don't think it could have entered his head. Of course he must have been annoyed at my father's long absence; he may even have found it surprising that my father had let a little thing like a general strike prevent him from getting home sooner. But after all, my father was grown up, I suppose the old man gave him credit for knowing what he was doing. Then why did the investigating commission put my grandfather into such a rage? I think it was just his dislike of officials and of having the authorities meddle in his private affairs. Anyway, that's how I look at it.

But let me go on with my father's criticism. Once he'd started carping at my book, there was no stopping him. "And what you say about Bahrenfeld—you really could have asked me first. It wouldn't have interfered with your scientific eyewash. I've read it carefully—everything you've written about Bahrenfeld and the army post—and I can't seem to get it straight. I keep thinking it couldn't have been the way you say, there must be something wrong. Good Lord, I certainly ought to know all about Bahrenfeld, the old barracks and Luruper Feld and the rifle range and the road to the railroad station. For five months they chased me around that place—before we were shipped out to Beverloo in Belgium and on to the front. No, your description isn't clear. Not a word, for instance, about the stables on the west side with the little opening at the top of the stalls where we'd let down the hay and oats for the horses. The work was back-breaking. And always getting chewed out. And me being from Uelzen, all I heard was, 'Get in there and scrub their rear ends.' That's right, Mother, don't turn up your nose, that's the way it was. Of course I know how to handle horses, any kid from Uelzen knows about horses, but I could think of better ways of spending my time.

"Maybe nobody else would notice that something is missing; I suppose other people find it interesting enough as it is. Let me tell you something, my boy, and don't be offended, I'm only your old father. I don't talk much about the old days. What for? Take when one of my friends at the hotel table asks me, Hey, Kurt, do you remember this or that? Of course I remember, does he think I'm stupid? But what's the good of warming up old soup, where does it get you? I have plenty of other things to think about. With you it's different, I know that. You're a history teacher and you're expected to teach the children all those things. I won't find fault with that, I wouldn't dare, but don't be offended, isn't your story kind of involved? I read it and reread it, and I can't help thinking that maybe what really happened was simpler. No, don't interrupt me, I'm not as dumb as I look. I'm aware of all the records you've quoted, all those documents and things, and the old newspaper clippings. You must have had a lot of trouble collecting all that stuff, anyone can see that. But take the newspaper clippings. Are they true? Everybody knows how people shoot off their mouths when something unusual is going on. A reporter hears some talk, and right away the papers print it, so we can read it next morning. And then somebody who was there comes along and says, It wasn't like that at all, I ought to know because I was in the thick of it. If you go by what it says in the paper, you're sunk. Would you expect me to pay attention to what the paper says about rebuilding my store? I don't even listen to Mother, who's against it, aren't you, Mother?—And take the pictures in your book. Don't be offended, but they're not good enough. If nothing better was available after all these years, I'd have dropped the pictures. But at least you could have put in a map of Hamburg, the section around the Rathaus where it all started, and maybe one of Bahrenfeld to show how those right-wing good-for-nothings were able to slip away in the dead of night to Eidelstedt and Oldesloe. The Hamburg people know their city, they don't need a map, but how can anyone else be expected to understand without even knowing which way north and south is. And then this famous Hein of yours! It's impossible, I just don't get it. I was in Hamburg while the shooting was going on, it's no secret. Well, what do you think your old father was doing all that time—sleeping? People shooting off guns in a big city—that doesn't happen every day. It's the kind of thing that interests an old soldier; naturally he looks around. Later on I showed Mother all the places where things were happening. Our trip to Hamburg was kind of a second honeymoon. Oh yes, it was, Mother. Because the first one, after the war, didn't amount to much. We only got as far as the Göhrde. Pudripp was the name of the village, remember, Mother? The featherbeds in the old inn were kind of skimpy. But we were young, we took long walks through the woods. Mother was always afraid we'd be attacked by wild boars, but we didn't see any. And that old pastor with his big hat! Why not, Mother? Why shouldn't I tell the children? It's no disgrace. This old geezer was always sitting around in the taproom. Mother and I had been walking all morning, so after lunch we lay down for a while. When we came down the stairs, the pastor was sitting there. 'Little afternoon nap?' he asks. Mother nods. 'Splendid!' he says. 'He who sleepeth sinneth not.' You should have seen Mother! The insolent lout! And that man calls himself a pastor! Isn't that just what happened, Mother? Why deny it? The trip to Hamburg was different. I showed her all the places. We took the Alster steamer to the Uhlenhorst ferry house, and then we had a boat ride around the harbor. Well anyway, I knew my way around from my days as a recruit, so wherever they were shooting I went and had a look. That makes me an eyewitness, so to speak. You really should have asked me about it beforehand, my boy, your book would have been a lot more precise. Take the picture of the Rathaus. The building looked pretty funny at the time, but you don't see that in the picture. It looked like it had smallpox; the brown sandstone was covered with white pimples, where bullets had struck. I suppose they patched it up, or maybe the grime just evened out the spots. And believe it or not, I even went out to Bahrenfeld to see the old barracks. It wasn't easy because nothing was running, but I had plenty of time and good young legs. Really, those white spots on the Rathaus would have looked good in your book; they're part of the story. One thing I can't understand is why I didn't see your famous Hein in those two weeks, because I

saw everything else. If as you say he was the strategic
genius that got the whole shebang moving, it seems to
me I'd have noticed him, because then he'd have been
in all the places where something was going on, and
those were just the places I went to. Don't be offended,
my boy, but it all looks kind of fishy, in spite of the
newspaper articles and the photographs. All right, I
won't say a word about your Hein, he was a little fellow,
but the big fellow, what was his name again . . . ?"

"Klaus Hundewatt."

"Funny names they've got in Hamburg. All right, I
might have overlooked your Hein in the confusion, but
how could I overlook a strategic genius? No, a strategic
genius would have caught my eye. And here on this
page it says the little runt suddenly turned up and
nobody knew where he came from and nobody knows
to this day, though he was a strategic genius. I know
everything was topsy-turvy, but that doesn't seem
possible. And then you say your Hein spoke Platt.
Or at least that other people who were there said so.
All right, a lot of people speak Platt. But I ask you,
what kind of Platt? Hamburg Platt or Uelzen Platt?
Not a word about that in your book, though the answer
would tell us where he came from. We can hear it a
mile away. Sometimes a man comes into the store and
starts talking Platt. I says to myself, Who's he trying
to fool? I bet you come from Dannenberg or Hitzacker,
sounds like Mecklenburg to me. See what I mean?
Don't bother me with your Platt. Does it prove that

your man's a strategic genius? Any clown can talk Platt, and this joker in the picture with the overgrown helmet looks like a clown to me; if he turned up in my store, I wouldn't trust him across the street. An unknown hero with his helmet down over his nose! Don't be offended, but he's just kidding around with your revolution. Mother is right, this clown in the steel helmet could just as well be me. I'll show you."

Whereupon my father goes over to the sideboard. As long as anybody can remember there's been an enormous punch bowl on it that's never been used, a hideous monstrosity, gray and blue earthenware. God knows how it ever got into our house. Some kind of anniversary present, I suppose. Even I was so used to seeing it that something would have seemed wrong if it hadn't been there. He claps the bowl on his head and comes to attention. Naturally my mother lets out a scream. "Well," he says, "here's your unknown hero!"

We had a good laugh. Beg your pardon? Yes, he took us in by showing us the truth. Precisely. We were all in stitches.

But wait. The best is yet to come. No sooner has my mother rescued her precious bowl and put it back on the sideboard than my father starts in again with his "Let me tell you something, my boy.

"I've been pacing the floor with your book—ask Mother if you don't believe me—trying to figure out what really happened, because all this historical business is for historians, it takes more education than

I ever had. And all these documents, as you call them, came later. Oh yes. When something's going on, nobody's got time for documents and suchlike. But then, when it's all over, they start writing articles for the papers; in other words, documents. Naturally an old Uelzen shopkeeper is going to scratch his head and wonder how it all started and what happened before the documents. So I put on my little thinking cap and tried to picture it, all the while checking the dates and street names and so on in your book. I've got to get those things right because there's no other way of proving that I know what I'm talking about. If any of my details are wrong, people will say my whole story is a fraud and I'm crazy. But if the details are right, they finally admit, Yes, Kurt, it sounds reasonable enough; that's the way it must have been. Not that I talk about these things to anybody else, no fear of that, I'm only saying this to you, because I wouldn't want you to think your old father was making fun of your book. The book is splendid, I have no fault to find with it, and if anybody starts running it down to me, I'll give him what for. My problem is that I want to understand it myself. So I've been thinking about your unknown Hein, because he's the main character in the book and because it seems pretty weird that I never caught sight of him during those days in Hamburg. Maybe it was pure chance; maybe I just didn't look in the right places because something was going on somewhere else, and then when I did look, your Hein was gone. I won't say

71

it's not possible, but it is peculiar. And since you haven't told us anything definite about your Hein, I mean, you only tell us what your documents say but not who he really was, and since nobody knows where the little runt turned up from all of a sudden or where he suddenly disappeared to, I figured that the best way to find out about this Hein would be to imagine that I was him and ask myself what I would have done. I decided to begin at the beginning and go on step by step and check every step against your book. And not to make him any dumber than myself, that would be a mistake, same as it's a mistake in business, because the man certainly wasn't dumb. So I toted your book around and put myself into his shoes, because I was really curious to know how a fellow like that gets into a revolution, with all that shooting and capturing the Rathaus, and how he came to have his picture taken in that steel helmet, because I figured there must be a good reason, and if I took my time and went about it right, I'd find out the reason, because this fellow couldn't have been very different from me and would probably act the same as I would. Naturally I didn't expect to come up with any historical truth, but there's no need of it, because you've got that in your book. But there'd be a kind of truth, the kind that simple people like me understand. I was all steamed up about it, because getting into a revolution and capturing a whole Rathaus is no joke; if things had gone wrong, and they easily could have, your man would have been stood up against the wall with the rest of them. Now at least I know the truth about your Hein, so I can sleep again. It doesn't affect your book in any way, my boy; my ideas are all about what isn't in your book. Well, if you're interested, I'll be glad to tell you my story. All right, just imagine that I'm your Hein."

But at this point my mother interrupted him. "It's all a lot of nonsense, Father, I know you inside out. Do you have to bore the children with such poppycock at their party?"

"You be still, Mother. Maybe it is stuff and nonsense, I won't argue with you about that. What I say is that you have all the rest of your lives to talk about the wedding and the household furnishings and which linen you're handing on to the children, but a book like this isn't written every day. You've got to take a little interest in it because your son wrote it, and if you don't he'll think his old parents are too stupid to care about such things. And a revolution may be nonsense, but it's something that doesn't happen every day—ask our boy, who's made a study of it. Just give the children some cake to keep up their strength."

What could my mother do in the face of such an appeal? Especially since my fiancée, just to be polite, said she would be fascinated to hear how my father pictured it all. And me? I was feeling too superior for words and looking forward to the fun. What do you think of that? A historian who hears the truth and mistakes it for light entertainment! We can all make mis-

73

takes? Very kind of you. But it doesn't matter. That was nearly twenty years ago; my stupidity doesn't worry me any more. What still troubles me a little is the figure of my father performing—yes, what else could you call it?—for an audience of three all leaning back comfortably in our chairs, sipping our wine, relating an episode in his life in the most inconceivable detail. Isn't that a terrifyingly lonely figure?

But enough of that. Sentimental self-reproach won't help any. Listen to my father instead. If nothing else, he was wittier.

"Well, children, this is the way it must have been. I spend the night at the hotel near the station. A small hotel, it burned down in the last war. I put on my good shirt because I was going to call on those big business-men and I wanted to make a good impression because of our credit standing. I go down to the breakfast room for my coffee, and I ask the man at the reception desk, 'what's that odd noise here in Hamburg?' And right away he starts whining. 'Why, they're shooting, Herr Hinrichs. They've been at it for hours. How were you able to sleep? It started right here on Steindamm and around the post office. Now it's over by the Rathaus, I think. I should have been relieved long ago, but none of the staff has shown up, and there's no coffee for you either. Myohmyohmy, what's to become of us, Herr Hinrichs?'

"'What are they shooting for?' I ask. 'Target practice?'

"'It's about the brawn, Herr Hinrichs. And there are no newspapers either.'

"You mentioned the business about the brawn in your book, so it must be true. Only I hadn't heard anything about it because I was sound asleep.

"Yes, Mother, just imagine, I'll tell you because you haven't read the book. It seems that some pork butcher in Barmbeck, that's a working-class neighbourhood in Hamburg, we didn't visit it on our trip, ground up rats in his brawn."

"Goodness gracious!"

"That's my own feeling. It still backs up on me when somebody asks for brawn in our store. I always expect a rat's tail to come popping out, though we sell only the very best quality, pure unadulterated pork. Well, in Hamburg they'd just heard about this brawn with the rats in it. Big excitement! This is how the government treats the workers and poor people! And then they started shooting. Maybe somebody'd made it up and it was only a pretext for getting the revolution started. You doubt the story in your book, son, and I think you're right. Being in the food business. Of course rats are plentiful. There are millions and millions of them. But how is anyone going to catch enough rats at one time to make it worthwhile to use them for brawn? It would cost him a pretty penny. No, somebody must have thought it up to make the women so mad they'd stir up the men. In that case they succeeded. Anyway, they started shooting.

"Well, don't let it spoil your appetite. There was nothing I could do to help this hotel clerk, who had his pants full. I guess he hadn't been in the war, he looked consumptive. So I just say, 'All right, give me my bill, I need it for my tax statement.' And he says, 'But you can't go home, Herr Hinrichs, the trains aren't running on account of the strike.' And I say, 'Let me worry about that, there must be some way.' So I pay for the one night and I leave my bag. He says he can't guarantee its safety in these unsettled times. On my way out, I can still hear him whining, 'What's to become of us, Herr Hinrichs!'

"And out I go. At the station there's really nothing doing. The ticket windows are all closed and so are the gates. Crowds of people are standing around with their baggage, griping and trying to find out how long it will be. Nobody's there to give out any information, not a uniform in sight. I listen a while, and then I say to myself, What's the use of standing around in this poultry yard, that's not what I came to Hamburg for. So I go out the other end of the station and listen to the shooting to see where it's coming from. Which is exactly what your Hein must have done, you can bet your bottom taler.

"Then I rummage in my pockets and find the slip of paper with the addresses of the people I'm supposed to see. All right, I says to myself, that's my next move, because shooting or not, that's what I came to Hamburg and put on my good shirt for. So I walk down this big street that leads to the Lombard Bridge, because I'd looked at the map and the nearest one of the addresses is right around the corner on Alsterdamm. It was a big import house; my father had told me all about it. Sure enough, the minute I turn the corner I see a doorway with the name of my firm on it and which floor it's on. The shooting's a good deal louder now. They must have had machine guns, I could tell. In a big city like that, they sound like carpet beating at spring-cleaning time.

"I start into the building, but I don't get very far. A man starts yelling at me, he's hopping mad. Must be the janitor. He's rolling garbage cans back into the building from the street, and I can see they're full. 'What do you want?' he yells at me. I tell him politely that I've come to see so and so on the second floor and he should kindly let me in. 'The building is closed,' he shouts. 'The gentlemen aren't working today. Make yourself scarce!' I thank him for the information, and to calm him down I ask, 'What are you hauling them back inside for? They haven't been emptied yet.' That makes him really mad; he thinks I'm making fun of him, but I was only trying to be friendly. 'You want to put up a barricade?' he yells at me. 'No,' I say, 'I'd only get dirty.' So then he tells me they'd tried to make off with his garbage cans to make a barricade with. 'They can kiss my ass with their barricade. Not with my garbage cans when I know the garbage men are on strike.' Yes, that's how it must have been. That's the way it goes in a revolution.

"So I go down Alsterdamm; it's really a nice-looking street, you'll have to admit it, Mother. All the fine shop windows full of cars and ladies' fashions, and on the other side the Inner Alster, as they call it, and the Alster steamboats. No, I don't think there were any steamboats that day, they must have been on strike too, but it's a nice-looking street all the same. I bet your unknown Hein liked it too, as he walked along, because, as you say in your book, he wasn't a Hamburg man, and a street like that looks pretty good to an out-of-towner. The weather? Now, let me see, what was the weather like? I've completely forgotten. To tell you the truth, son, you should have said something about the weather; it's important on a day like that when they're making a revolution. Anyway, it wasn't raining, I'd have remembered that because of my good suit.

"So this Hein of yours is strolling down Alsterdam and probably thinking to himself, Why not take a look at the shooting? He must have, because that's what I was thinking; you always feel that way when something's going on and you haven't anything else to do. Suppose somebody asks you later on, What? You were there and you didn't bother to watch? You'd be embarrassed.

"Of course there wasn't as much traffic as usual on Alsterdamm. A few people were running back and forth along the housefronts, waving their arms and shouting, Don't go any farther. They're shooting. Hm, thank you kindly, I can hear for myself that they're shooting.

"At Alstertor there's quite a crowd; the shooting at the Rathaus couldn't reach them because of the houses in between. They've brought in a woman who's been hit. At first I thought she'd passed out from the excitement and I might as well go on; there were plenty of women around her, wailing and hollering for a doctor. But I was mistaken. They turned her over on her belly and I saw she'd been hit in the rear end; the bullet had gone clear through one buttock and it was a pretty fat rear end."

"So of course you took a good look at it," says my mother disgustedly.

"Well, Mother, our friend Hein certainly took a look at it, and if you ask me, he was right. After all, he was an old soldier, it says so here in the book, and a man with his experience knows all about wounds, so maybe he could have helped. But I see at a glance that they don't need me. It's only a flesh wound; maybe they'll have to cut out a chunk of flesh, but who'll notice it back there? Of course she's bleeding like a stuck pig and the women are stuffing all kinds of rags into the wound to stop the blood. And you never heard such screaming. Well, I says to myself, I might as well be going, they can handle that by themselves. You'll have to admit, Mother, it's often the wrong people that get hit in a revolution. The same in war. Nobody ever thinks of writing a book about the wrong people, but you can't help feeling sorry for them. This poor woman certainly had nothing to do with the revolution;

79

anyway, she didn't look it, though all I saw of her was her rear end, and now she's running around with a scar, which embarrasses her because of her fiancé. You could have put in a paragraph about that, son. If you ask me—don't be offended—it would have improved your book.

"Well, as I say, it was none of my business, so your Hein trots along, following the sound of the shooting. That's the simplest way in a city you don't know. There's quite a racket as I come closer, but I was used to much worse from the war; a little thing like that doesn't cut much ice with an old soldier. Of course, I listen to find out what direction most of the shooting is coming from, so as not to get into the thick of it. You do that out of old habit, and in time you develop a pretty good ear.

"So I come to the corner where Alsterdamm ends. There's a big café on that corner, I forget what it's called. Some of the windowpanes have been smashed, the pieces are all over the street. It must have cost them a pile of money, because it's a safe bet that the insurance company wouldn't pay. Rotten luck. Inside the café the chairs are still on the tables; they haven't even opened because of the shooting. But there are people. They've crawled under the tables, and they motion to me and point in the direction of the Rathaus, to warn me not to go any farther but to crawl in with them. That's what I understand at least; I couldn't make out what they were yelling because of the noise. Nothing doing, friends, what am I going to do in your café when there isn't even any coffee? Besides, I've got to economize, I haven't got much money. But thanks all the same.

"Because I've seen something that interests me a good deal more. Right across the street. I can't believe my eyes."

"Another naked lady's rear end?" my mother asks.

"No, Mother, something even more interesting. As I've already told you, my boy, it's really a pity you didn't put a map of the city in your book. At least a little one of the neighborhood around the Rathaus. Then I could show you much more clearly how in my modest opinion it must have been. Who can remember the names of all these streets in a strange city? The one on the right is Jungfernstieg, any child who's been to Hamburg knows that, but what was the name of the Street that comes down from the Petrikirche?

"Well, it can't be helped. I'll have to manage without a map. Here where I'm putting the book down is the corner with the café, and this glass is where I'm standing. The Alster and Jungfernstieg are on the right, but that doesn't matter, and here in front is the street I don't remember the name of. And now pay attention. Right across from the café and from where I'm standing there's a little side street, a very short one, and looking down it, I can see the Rathaus. You follow me? The name of this little street is the Plan; I remember it because the street sign caught my attention when I was standing there later on. You've mentioned the street in your book and you've got it right. Funny street names they've got in Hamburg, but they must know that themselves. The Siechen Beer Hall is on the corner of this little street; Mother and I had lunch there, do you remember, Mother? You were crazy about the sauerkraut.

"And what do I see? No, it's impossible! I look again, I look three times, and by golly across from Siechen's they've got a field gun. Five or six fellows bustling around it, trying to aim it at the Rathaus. They haven't the faintest idea what they're doing. Naturally, an old field-artillery man can see that at a glance. At that point there's no holding your Hein. Take my word for it. It would have been the same with me.

"I cross the street and look on. For a while I just stand around and nobody says anything, because they're all much too excited, like children with a toy they don't know how to work. When I get in their way, they just shove me aside. So I step into the nearest doorway, so as not to interfere with them, and also because of the shooting. This street, you see, was straight in the line of fire from the Rathaus. True, there's not much coming in this direction, they must be shooting somewhere else, over by Mönckebergerstrasse and the Old Wall and the Alster Arcades, and behind the Rathaus near the Stock Exchange. But now and then a bullet comes whizzing down the Plan, the mean kind that ricochets off the pavement and buzzes around your ears like a horsefly. They make holes that can't be darned. There's no sense in standing there playing the hero, so I step back a little way into the doorway, I can see just as well from there. I see by the signs on the walls to the right and left of me that the building is all full of lawyers' offices, and I wonder why lawyers should have picked this particular building. And what else do I see? A laundry basket. And in that laundry basket a dozen little shells to go with the gun. Can you imagine? A plain ordinary laundry basket with the name of the laundry written on one side. It's more than I can take. Some soldiers you turned out to be! But naturally I didn't say it out loud, because people get excited in a revolution and that can lead to misunderstandings.

"So I go on watching them, and naturally I notice this big fellow, your Hundewatt, as you call him. He's the ringleader, that's plain, and the way he was cursing—magnificent. A fine brute of a man, your picture is all right. He could have carried the whole gun on his back; it was only a small field gun, nothing to write home about, but all the same, it had a big armorplate shield to protect the gunner, and that alone must have weighed a hundred pounds. You could work up quite a sweat with one of those guns, and your Hundewatt is trying so hard, it's flowing down in rivers. He keeps pushing and pulling it around, fiddling with the breech lock and twisting the sight in his big fist like a wild man. I'm afraid he's going to break it off. It's no use, Fatso, you'll never get that breech open with those sausage fingers, strength won't do it. It's easy as pie if you know how, I could do it in my sleep. That's what I'm thinking, and I stand there grinning, because I'm thinking of the army post and the way they drilled us, and the war and all.

"Well, Hundewatt just happens to look up and see me grinning. I was just unlucky. If you ask me, your Hein was the unlucky kind. Because if the dope hadn't grinned, everything would have turned out different and you wouldn't have had to write your book. Well, it can't be helped. We're all of us unlucky sometimes.

"Your Hundewatt jumps up. He's good and mad. He was mad to begin with because he wasn't getting anywhere with the gun. His face is so red I expect him to explode. He comes lurching over to me, swinging those big brawny arms. There are two others with him. One has his rifle slung over his shoulder, but with the barrel down, that's the style in revolutions because it's forbidden in the army, and the other has two hand grenades in his belt. Well, I says to myself, this doesn't look too good, I'd better take it easy.

"'Hey, you,' Hundewatt yells at me, 'what's so funny?' In Platt of course, even if it is only Hamburg Platt. That made me feel a little better. 'Are you asking for a punch in the nose?'

"'Nope,' I say in my good old Uelzen Platt. 'It would spoil my Sunday suit.'

"'Then beat it in your Sunday suit,' he bellows. What a voice he had; they could shoot all they pleased,

84

I heard him all right. 'We don't need anybody grinning around here when other people are knocking themselves out. Take him away, comrades, we'll attend to him later. He looks like a reactionary to me. All right, take him away!'

"I wasn't very happy. In these revolutions you never know what can happen to you because people get so excited. The others are poking me, they want me to come along, so I ask him quick, 'Are you trying to fire that thing?'

"You should have seen him. I thought he was going up in the air like a bomb. 'What do you expect us to do with it? Clean out your bowels?'

"'Nope,' I say. 'I can see it's a plain ordinary field gun, and those shells in your laundry basket are just the right caliber.'

"'Wait a second, comrades,' he yells. And to me, 'Do you know anything about it?'

"'I'd be some sap if I didn't, they drummed it into me for four years.'

"'Can the thing be fired?'

"'Of course it can, if it's not stuffed up. And if you haven't broken the breech lock.'

"'Can it hit the Rathaus?'

"'Why not? It's not three hundred yards. It'll carry that far.'

"'Can it be aimed?'

"'That's what the sights are for that you almost broke off.'

"'And will those eggs explode?'

"'Why shouldn't they? They look fresh to me. Better not take a hammer to them, they're sensitive. Where'd you get all these toys?'

"He scratches his head and looks at his comrades. A decent sort, I can see that, only too strong for his own good and so excited about his revolution. And now he's feeling foolish because he yelled at me and told them to take me away.

"'You see, I was in the navy,' he says. 'And I worked only in the engine room. If you could show us how to fire this thing at those pigs in the Rathaus . . .'

"'Pigs?'

"'Reactionary dogs. White pigs! They're shooting at us, so we want to shoot back. If you could show us . . .'

"'Of course I'll show you. Why not?'

"'The revolution will thank you to your dying day,' he says.

"'No need of thanks,' I say. 'It's easy.'

"'All right, then let's go. Make way,' he commanded. 'The comrade's going to show us.'"

You should have heard my mother. She was so indignant she popped up from her chair. "What? He had the nerve to call you comrade?" And we had another big laugh.

"Think nothing of it, Mother. They're always calling him 'Comrade Hein' in the book, though all we know of him is that he was in the field artillery. Am I right, son? That's the way it is. Soldiers call each other buddy,

86

and in a revolution they call each other comrade. It's always been that way and doesn't mean a thing, it's just the custom. Look at it this way, Mother: the way I'm telling it, the story is pretty slow and long-winded, but the way it really happened, there was no time for company manners. People were shooting and we had to hurry. If your Comrade Hein was really an artillery-man, it must have given him a big kick to show the boys his stuff. I'd have been the same; it would have made my fingers itch to see how they were bungling it.

"Well, just to be on the safe side, I look through the barrel to make sure those idiots hadn't stuffed anything into it that would make the whole gun explode in our noses. Then I tell them to take hold, because we've got to block the carriage. They'd never thought of that; the recoil would have sent it rolling clear across the square to the Alster. We couldn't ram the trail spike into the ground because of the cobblestones, so I tell them we'll have to back her up against the lamppost and block the wheels with cobblestones. The way they obeyed me was a pleasure, especially big Hundewatt. Obliging fellows, really decent. When we've wedged it into place, I sit down on the carriage the way I'd learned to do. One of the boys hands me an egg and I load it; it takes half a second when you know how. Then I ask Hundewatt, 'Well, comrade, what do you want me to shoot at?'"

Again my mother makes a face, as if she'd swallowed the wrong way, and my father had to explain that he had no choice because he didn't yet know the man's name was Hundewatt, and even if he had known, he couldn't very well have said at a time like that, If you please, Herr Hundewatt, what do you wish? It wasn't the same as talking to a customer in the store.

"Hundewatt yells, 'At the balcony of course!'

"'Why the balcony?'

"'Because that's where they've got their machine gun, you fool; that's why we're not getting anywhere.'

"I can't see the machine gun, and at the moment it's not firing. Maybe they're saving ammunition, it's possible, or maybe it's jammed. The old machine guns we had in those days were always jamming and, boy, did the gunners curse. It seems they've invented better ones since.

"But of course I can see the balcony. What a shame, I says to myself, wrecking that fine ironwork. I've shown you the balcony, Mother. And in taking aim there's something else to consider. I'll have to shoot right past old Kaiser Wilhelm's head. In those days, you see, he was still sitting there on his green horse, gazing at the Rathaus, all quiet and peaceful as if there hadn't been any revolution or any shooting. I don't want to shoot the old man's head off, that wouldn't be right, and your Comrade Hein wouldn't have done it either. In the meantime they've moved the whole monument somewhere else; they needed the square for parking, but then it was straight in the line of fire.

"'Can't you make it?' Hundewatt yells. He doesn't

know anything about aiming a gun and can't see why
I'm hesitating.

"'Of course I can make it.'

"'Then fire, for God's sake, man!' It's amazing how
jittery a giant like that can be.

"Well, at that moment the idiots in the Rathaus
begin firing their machine gun; they've fixed it, and
maybe they've spotted us, because the bullets came
splashing down on our street, they hit a windowpane
above us, and the glass comes tumbling down on our
heads. Nobody likes that kind of thing. It makes me
mad, so I give them one.

"I knew my business. Not a bad shot, I don't mind
telling you. A little too far to the right, but that's only
because of the old Kaiser's head, and maybe a yard too
high. It hit the pillar next to their balcony window, but
it must have given them a good scare.

"'Another!' Hundewatt yells, and hands me another
shell out of the laundry basket. This time I hit the
balcony grating square. That does it!

"'More!' the comrades yell. But then I go on strike.

"I stand up behind my shield. 'Nothing doing. Why
ruin their expensive building?' Anyway there was no
need to, nobody was firing from up there any more; I
guess there wasn't much left of their machine gun.
Instead of machine-gun fire we hear shouting from the
other streets that we couldn't see; obviously they were
storming the Rathaus.

"And just for the hell of it, and because it was what

they had taught us to do in an emergency, I sing out, 'The company will take orders from me!'

"It worked; by that time they regarded me as an authority. Hundewatt picks up the gun, so to speak. I mean he harnesses himself up front and the other comrades push from behind. And away we go on the double. Not exactly regulation style, but this was a revolution. We couldn't go straight across because of the monument and the steps it was standing on, so we gallop around the Rathaus market. Your Hundewatt keeps bellowing, 'Make way, comrades. Make way for the artillery!' And two of the comrades come puffing along after us with the laundry basket. We're in a hurry because we want to be in on the storming of the Rathaus.

"My idea is to set the gun up close by in case they need us to breach the main gate. Man alive, did we sweat, but by the time we get there, we're not needed. They're hanging a tablecloth out of a window beside the balcony. A crying shame, Mother; genuine damask, fifteen or twenty feet long, with the arms of Hamburg woven in. In a big Rathaus like that, they've got nothing but the best. They must have just taken it out of the cupboard, because you can still see the creases, and it's starched too. Well, let's hope they took it in after a while and sent it to the laundry.

"So it was all over and the Rathaus had been stormed. No more shooting, just a little back by the Stock Exchange. I guess the people behind the Rathaus didn't know about the tablecloth. Later on, the young scamps who'd gone on shooting were driven into the canal. What you say about it in your book is correct, and it wasn't nice; they kept shooting at them while they were swimming around. What would you expect in the excitement? The youngsters themselves were to blame; why did they have to play hero? No real soldier does that. That's the first thing you learn at the front, nobody has to teach you; you just find out that nothing but trouble comes of it.

"Well, when it's all over, the newspapermen come along with their cameras. They want to take pictures of the gun, because they've heard that we're responsible for the victory and it wouldn't have gone so quickly and smoothly without us. And what do you know? They've already got a red flag flying from the balcony. God only knows where they found it in such a hurry. And they're standing up there singing the *Internationale*. Naturally we join in the singing and raise our clenched fists. That was the thing to do. That's how it is in a revolution, Mother, you can't sing 'Deutschland, Deutschland,' it's not the custom, but there's got to be singing because a victory calls for a celebration. Comrade Hein must have picked up a steel helmet, you always find those things lying around, and just for the fun of it or to make us look military while we're having our pictures taken, Hundewatt claps the steel chamber pot on his head. Which explains how this funny-looking object got into the picture and into your book.

"Yes, my boy, that's how a Rathaus gets captured; it's not nearly as complicated as your book would lead people to think. All you need is one man who knows how to handle a field gun; that's all there is to it, the rest takes care of itself. I'm only telling you all this because I can't see how your Comrade Hein could have acted any different. He seems to have had a head on his shoulders, and besides, what else could he have done? Of course, my idea isn't scientific, I'm aware of that."

My mother was in a pretty bad humor. To her it was all "stuff and nonsense." "No wonder," she says contemptuously. "No wonder you got axle grease all over your good suit."

"Yes, Mother, that could be, because you've got to keep those guns coated with grease or they rust. But on the other hand, if this Hein was an artilleryman, he must have known about the grease and taken care. Even uniformed soldiers aren't supposed to get themselves all full of grease every time they handle a gun—some chewing-out they'd get.—Well, children, now let's talk about my building plans and your engagement."

We could have stopped there; my father seemed to have no desire to comment any further on my book. If he kept on, I have only myself to thank. Today I find it hard to understand what got into me. To call a spade a spade, I suppose my trouble was author's vanity. I guess I was itching to trip my father up, to rehabilitate my book by exposing some discrepancy between his fantasies and the historical facts. Stupid of me! That's all I can say today. My only excuse is that as I've said before, my father's Uelzen Platt made everything he told us sound like a sweet little fairy tale.

Can you imagine, I even told him so at the time. I complimented him. "You described it all so well that I can see it. Why, it's as if you'd been there yourself. For instance, those lawyers' nameplates there on the doorway. That's marvelous. It passed before my eyes like a movie."

What a simpleton I was, complimenting my father as a teacher might compliment a student who had turned in a good essay. My father was very modest about it; he declined the compliment. "But, my boy, I saw those signs. I pointed them out to Mother before we went to Siechen's for lunch. Remember, Mother? They were really there; maybe they are still, if the building wasn't blown up in the Second World War. In that case, of course, the lawyers have gone somewhere else."

"I only meant that you made it so vivid, Father. What an imagination you've got!"

"No, son, there's no imagination to it. It's all out of your book or suggested by what isn't in your book. I read it and read it again, and I asked myself, Isn't there some gap here? Of course there's a gap, and it's not your fault, because when something happens and you haven't any documents to help you, there's bound to be a gap. All you can do is wait for another document to turn up, and then you go on writing. I realize that when you fellows write a historical book you've got to do it that way, but the gaps are very interesting to somebody like me. I stop and scratch my head and ask myself, Now what can have happened at this point? Maybe it was something very important, even if there aren't any documents. So then I put myself in the gap and try to figure out what your Hein or your Hundewatt was up to. That's not imagination."

Here my mother threw in another of her peevish remarks: "You've always been a deep thinker. I'll thank my Maker if there isn't some gap in these building plans of yours and we don't all tumble into it."

How we laughed, and most of all my father. "Take it easy, Mother. Let me explain this thing about gaps. Remember that little incident on our wedding day— there are no documents about it, but you can't claim it didn't happen. All right, children, I'll tell you about it. We'd just come out of the church and gotten into the carriage to drive to the Fischerhof for our wedding lunch—Grandpa had insisted on the Fischerhof, he didn't care for the Hotel Stadt Hamburg; too fancy, he said—well, we're driving along, you and me up front with the dapple grays and all the flowers on the rack, and then in the next carriage my parents and your father, and then the pastor with his stuck-up wife who was always poking her nose into other people's affairs, and then the bridesmaids and the other guests; it was a big wedding, you can't deny it. Well, all of a sudden I see this pinch of salt plucking at her bouquet and her veil and wriggling in her seat—yes, Mother, you may as well admit it, that's just what you were doing—and I ask her, 'What are you so nervous about, little girl?' And she says in her peppery way, 'Nervous? The idea! I'm not nervous.' 'Oh yes, you are,' I say. 'We're married now, so you may as well tell me what's wrong.' 'Well,' she says, 'I have to go to the toilet.' It was quite a problem. We couldn't stop the carriage with that cavalcade behind us, and she couldn't simply get out in the middle of the park in her white dress. Well, we made it all right to the Fischerhof and nobody noticed anything. I'm only saying that this toilet business might have ruined our whole wedding. Which reminds me, Mother, there's something I haven't shown you in my plans. Here by the cellar steps we're installing a brand-new toilet, not for the personnel, they can use the old ones out in the yard, but to prevent a disaster in case one of our lady customers has to pee."

"You nasty man!" said my mother. "Do you have to talk about such things?" But she couldn't help laughing, because for all her straitlaced ways she had a sense of humor. The only one whose sense of humor was on the blink was me. I kept right at it.

"That's all very well and good, Father, and to judge by what I know about Comrade Hein, it may actually have been as you say. At least up to the storming of the Hamburg Rathaus. That I admit. But what happened then? The Rathaus was only the beginning and by no

95

means the most important part of the uprising, let's not forget that. If the revolution had ended with the Rathaus, we'd never have heard of Comrade Hein. If he came to be known as the 'Unknown Hero,' it's demonstrably because of the events that followed, from the bloodless capture of the Bahrenfeld army post to the brilliant feint in the direction of Magdeburg, which, as we know, was decisive. All the contemporary witnesses agree that the plan for that march on Magdeburg originated with Comrade Hein. Why should they have lied? They had no reason whatever to lie. Why should they have wanted to give a total stranger all the credit if it wasn't true? That would have been most unusual, and how would you account for it psychologically? In short, I believe that our likeliest hope of elucidating this unknown hero of ours lies in the subsequent events. And if this is true, we are confronted by two main questions: in the first place, it seems hard to believe that the initiators of the uprising, or to put it plainly, the Communist Party, should have entrusted the military leadership to a total stranger for no other reason than that he knew how to fire a field gun. Isn't it much more likely that the man wasn't a stranger at all and that if the Communists were so quick to accept his leadership in this critical situation, it was simply because he had previously been in contact with them, even if we have no documentary proof of it. The second question, which is related to the first and reinforces my supposition, is this: why did he go on fighting after the Rathaus was disposed of? On that point, Father, your imagination has tangled you up. You assume that he behaved as you would have done. You say the circumstances forced him to fire on the Rathaus, and that may be true. But once the Rathaus was taken, he hadn't the slightest reason to go on with it, or more specifically, to get involved in the Bahrenfeld venture. Yes, let's stick to Bahrenfeld for the moment. Between the storming of the Rathaus and the encirclement of the Bahrenfeld army post, at least twelve hours elapsed, more likely fourteen, and the executive committee, or whatever we choose to call the leadership of the uprising, had their hands full. During that time our man could have slipped away; nobody would have noticed and nobody would have cared. He could have vanished from the face of the earth, so to speak, as he actually did some days later. Can you explain why, instead of doing that, he marched along to Bahrenfeld?"

"For the fun of it, I guess."

"No, Father, I won't accept that as an answer. Fun isn't a serious argument."

"You're quite right. It's not serious."

"And after all, this Hein was no fool."

"No, he was no fool. Maybe he did it out of friendship for Hundewatt. He couldn't leave him in the lurch just like that."

"You see!" I triumphed. "You've tripped yourself up. In that case Hein must have been much more involved in the revolutionary movement than you suppose, because according to your account he'd only known Hundewatt for a few minutes. Friendships aren't made all that quickly."

"I don't agree. Men make friends very easily when the bullets are flying."

"That is insufficient explanation and you know it."

"You've become a great debater at the university. I can't keep up with you."

"I'm not trying to win a debate, Father. I'm only trying to make it clear to you that your theories are inadequate. They don't make Comrade Hein's participation in the Bahrenfeld expedition seem even halfway plausible."

"To tell you the truth," said my father with a sigh, "I didn't want to say anything about Bahrenfeld."

"You see!" Again I was triumphant.

Yes, triumphant. I thought I had defended my historian's honor against the fantasies of a layman and driven my father into a corner, when as a matter of fact he was only joshing me in the most good-natured way and even leaving me a possibility of retreat, because he didn't want to make me look like too much of a fool.

He sighed again and picked up the book. "Well, Mother, it can't be helped. We'll just have to talk about it if that's what your boy wants." Then he leafed through the book until he found the passage he wanted. "Here it is, on page 114. The only reason I don't like to talk about it is that I know Bahrenfeld too well from the days when I was stationed there, and I'm sorry because I don't like to make you feel badly. But the fact is, I don't like the chapter about Bahrenfeld at all —don't be offended, it really doesn't matter whether I like it or not. Here on page 114, you see, I was struck by another of these gaps. All right. Let's go back to page 113. We're standing outside the Rathaus, singing the *Internationale*. The red flag is hanging from the balcony, and you've got the picture in the right place too. But then you simply jump to page 114, you even leave half a page blank, and then the Bahrenfeld chapter begins. That won't do. You've left too much of a gap between 113 and 114. Bahrenfeld is quite a way from the Rathaus, you can't just jump. Even on the train it takes half an hour; I ought to know, because when we went out on pass we had to figure pretty close to be back on time, and even so we always had to run the last stretch, though it was forbidden to run in uniform, they said it made a bad impression. See what I mean? And in your book the trains weren't running. Even a man like your Hein couldn't jump from the Rathaus to Bahrenfeld. No, take my word for it. This gap between 113 and 114 is just too big. Something must have happened in that gap, even if there aren't any documents.

"For instance, the boys must have had something to eat. They couldn't very well march from the Rathaus to Bahrenfeld on an empty stomach and hold out till the following morning. You fellows never think of such things when you write your books. But a thing like that is important, even in a revolution. Let me tell you how I figure it, my boy. This document business of yours is all right, I won't say a word against it, but certain things must have happened all by themselves. They usually do, and it's only later on that somebody gets credit, though the whole thing just happened and he only took part in it because he had no choice. If this store here is being rebuilt and renovated, it's only because my father in his time rebuilt Grandfather's little shop and because the town is growing and automobiles are here to stay and conditions in Uelzen aren't what they were in my father's day. Like it or not, you've got to take such things into account and you don't need to be a genius; situations develop all by themselves, all you have to do is keep awake and move when the time is ripe. That's right, Mother, make faces if you must, but the time is ripe. I'm sure your Hein would have been glad to slip away after they'd taken his picture in the steel helmet, I can see that, but then things just happened, because even if I don't know as much about these revolutions as you do, what with your studies, I can easily imagine that even in a revolution a good many things just happen without benefit of strategic genius, as you call it. And even if you don't like the idea, I say the little runt must have been having fun, he looks like it to me. A revolution must have been kind of a change for him.

"All right. You tell us yourself on page 113 how they

made a big fuss over him and cheered him because he'd
fired the gun and the young scamps in the Rathaus were
so scared that they'd hung out the tablecloth. If it
hadn't been for him, it might have taken a good deal
longer and a lot more people would have been killed
too. Well, it's fun to be cheered for a thing like that,
and you yourself write that from then on they called
him Comrade Hein.

"And now this Bahrenfeld expedition. The idea came
all by itself. You even say so in your book, though you
misinterpreted the facts. You mention—let's see, what
page was it on?—a telegram from Berlin where the
revolution was going on too—why, there you have a
document. In this telegram the Berlin comrades warned
the Hamburg comrades that troops were on their way
from Bavaria, a free corps, as you call it. They're heavily
armed and they're marching on Magdeburg. And it
tells us we've got to help the Magdeburg people. That
must have put a crimp on their celebration. Here they'd
just been singing the *Internationale*, they hadn't even
had time to catch their breath, when this telegram
comes along and queers the whole picture. At a time
like that you can't just run away and let your friends
down; you must know that. I certainly wouldn't have
run away. Besides, it wasn't possible. You can be sure
they dragged me into their Rathaus, with or without
my steel helmet, I don't remember, to make a fuss over
me and thank me, and then they held a kind of council
of war about the telegram and Magdeburg and all, and

naturally I had to take part; they couldn't manage
without me because they all thought I knew more about
these things than they did. Yes, that's how I figure it
at least, and I'm sure it didn't happen very different.
Then at their council of war, when the leaders in their
horn-rimmed glasses were stymied, they probably asked
me, What do you think, Comrade Hein? How are you
going to answer a question like that if all you've got is
a little common sense and no special knowledge? Well,
my answer would have been: without arms it can't be
done, because those fellows from Bavaria are specialists,
you can't scare them with a small field gun. If you can't
rustle up some arms, you'd better drop the whole idea,
you wouldn't be doing the Magdeburg people any good.
Where are you going to get arms? You must know that
better than I do, comrades—now don't start making
faces again, Mother. How can I help calling them
'comrades'? I can't very well say 'ladies and gentlemen'—and anyway, there weren't any ladies.

"If you think yourself into the situation, you see that
the word Bahrenfeld must have come up, that somebody must have said there were arms there but that a
company of the young fellows we'd driven out of the
Rathaus had occupied the place. You mention that in
your book. Well, if your Hein had been in the field
artillery, he must have pricked up his ears at the word
Bahrenfeld. Certainly I would have. I'd have asked the
comrades if it was true, if there were still arms there, and
they probably would have answered yes, a whole pile

of them left over from the war and some vehicles too. And my next question, which is only logical, is: how many men occupied the post? They tell me—and they were just about right, I think—two hundred to two hundred and fifty, certainly no more, and all of them kids, papas' darlings. When you think of the circumstances, there was only one thing I could say, and I say it, All right, comrades, let's go, let's see if we can scare those kids away. Comrade Hundewatt slaps me on the back and yells, You're a good man, Comrade Hein, and I yell, Don't break my back with your big paw. If you want to do something, get us some flares. What for? he asks. Don't you know what they are? Or haven't you got any in Hamburg? And you know what? The guy's offended at me saying that about Hamburg. The rest of them look at Comrade Hein, and they think, Leave it to him, he knows what he's doing. That started them talking. One of them says they've got flares in the harbor in Warehouse No. So and so, and another says something about the Port Police and the Pilot Office and the Customs House. Still another remembers seeing some lying around the cellar of the old armory on Bundesstrasse. Well, that's their business. They send out the comrades, they beat it on the double, and I call after them, Get as much as you can, comrades, we need a whole pile, and make it quick. When they've gone, Hundewatt asks me, What are you going to do with the stuff? And I explain, It'll be dark by the time we get to Bahrenfeld. We'll give them a little display of fireworks.

"You see, my boy, there's room for a lot of ideas between page 113 and page 114. Later on in the chapter you describe the fireworks around the army post. Too bad there's no picture of it, a picture would have looked good in your book. Well, I'm reading about these fireworks and I can't help thinking there's something wrong here. Where did these flares come from all of a sudden? You don't just find those things lying around when you happen to need them. You try and pick up a supply of flares here in Uelzen, or in Celle for that matter, not to mention the big pistols you shoot them off with, because if you haven't got a pistol, you're likely to burn your fingers bad. Somebody must have hit on the idea between page 113 and page 114; maybe it was your Hein and maybe it was some other joker, that's not important. The important thing is that some of the comrades in Hamburg knew where to look for them and laid in a supply before we made that jump from the Rathaus to Bahrenfeld.

"Actually we didn't jump. The comrades requisitioned a lot of trucks, the place was full of idle trucks because of the strike, and in the end we had more than we needed. So we all pile in and start for Bahrenfeld. With red flags of course and plenty of yelling. We took the old field gun along too, in case we'd need it; anyway it was good propaganda, a thing like that always makes an impression. We didn't drive fast, we weren't in any hurry, because it had to be dark when we got there, and besides, we had to wait for the flares. It was a kind of propaganda parade for the benefit of the population. And you should have seen the crowd! Even without any newspapers, everybody knew what had happened, and they all shouted, Hurrah for Comrade Hein. By the time we got to Holsten Station, we had a thousand people with us, and more kept coming. There were women too, they had plenty of time on their hands with the strike. It's nice, I'm thinking, having all these people in the revolution, and Comrade Hundewatt's beaming from ear to ear, but it worried me too. Maybe they'd bottle us up, and besides, a crowd like that can only get in the way when you're attacking an army post. Suppose they start shooting from inside the post; it would be a disaster. A man doesn't have to be a genius, as you claim in your book, to see that.

"So I poke Comrade Hundewatt. He's standing beside me in the truck, waving at the crowd the whole time—I was mighty glad to have him there, because the people all knew him from meetings and he was very popular, and anyway you feel safer with a big bruiser like that—so I poke him and say, It's no good, comrade. He doesn't like that at all, he thinks we've won the revolution because all these people in the street are with us and Bahrenfeld will be a pushover with such a crowd. But I stick to my guns; I tell him it's looking for trouble and we don't want the comrades to get hurt. And anyway, we have to wait for the flares.

"Believe me, it's not so easy convincing a man like

that, but he finally sees my point. So we stop at a big building on the outskirts of Altona and set up a kind of headquarters. It turns out to be a school; there are school desks in all the rooms, but no teachers; I guess they were scared. Lucky the place was a school, because there was a big map of Hamburg on the wall, with Bahrenfeld and everything on it, for geography class, I suppose. Yes, even in a revolution you've got to have luck on your side. We had no map and a map was just what we needed.

"Naturally all the comrades who'd come along wondered what we were stopping for. I told Hundewatt he'd have to make a speech and explain, because we didn't want any disorder. I tell him what to say, and I stand beside him and prompt him when he gets stuck. Naturally I let him do the talking. With that chest of his, he's got a voice you can hear at the other end of town. There weren't any microphones in those days.

"So Hundewatt bellows across the square, so loud the windowpanes rattled, 'Comrades, Comrade Hein here, who took the Rathaus for us . . .' You should have heard the shouting. The people raised their fists and yelled, 'Heil Moscow!' and all the other things people shout at a time like that, and I smile and wave and motion them to calm down. Actually that shouting was a good thing, because they must have heard it in Bahrenfeld and I'll bet they had their pants full. Finally Hundewatt was able to go on. 'Comrade Hein here has a plan. He's worked out a way . . . of . . . of . . .'

'Crushing the class enemy,' I whisper. 'Crushing the class enemy,' he bellows across the square. 'We've only got to wait for ammunition; I've given orders and it'll be here soon. And besides, we don't want to get there until it's dark. We've got to do exactly what it says in Comrade Hein's plan; he figured it out and he's in command. We want that plan to work and to make it work we need . . . we need . . .' He couldn't find the right word and again I prompt him. '. . . Discipline. Yes, comrades, class discipline, that's what we need. And to make sure we get discipline, Comrade Hein has asked me to ask for volunteers. Anybody who's been in the army and knows about discipline can volunteer. Heil Moscow!'

"It was a fine speech, and you should have seen the volunteers crowding forward. They almost came to blows because they all wanted to enforce discipline, and most of the men had been in the army, there was no shortage. Well, that was a situation Comrade Hundewatt could take care of, he was made for it, and they all respected him. When the pushing got too bad, he just bellowed at them and order was restored. He asks them for their party cards and suchlike and shoots off his mouth about party discipline, that word seems to have made a big impression on him. I ask them about things like branch of service and what front they'd been on, because an old soldier knows the score without being told and he doesn't need any long speeches about discipline, he'll only feel insulted. So we choose twenty or thirty men, and I tell each one to pick a group they can rely on, as many as they like; the main thing is no nonsense and not to lift a finger without orders. Then I show them on the city map—yes, we'd spread it out on the table like my building plans here—I show each one of them where to go with his outfit and to wait till it's dark and for God's sake not to do anything on their own, I'm holding each one of them responsible, because that would wreck the whole plan, they should just wait for a courier to bring them orders. I tell them to take food and maybe something to drink in a vacuum flask. But they don't have to keep quiet, they can sing and make as much noise as they like. And I said I'd send them flares and the big pistols they'd need. Did they know how to handle them? Naturally old soldiers knew how to handle them, there's nothing to it anyway. They should send up a flare every few minutes and not try to economize. They promised to do what I said, and then I showed them on the map where our next command post would be, in a bar on the street that runs directly from the army post to the railroad station. Most of them knew the place, and of course I knew it from my days in Bahrenfeld. Then I asked Hundewatt if he could scare up some men with motorcycles, and he had them for me in a minute, a bunch of young fellows who get a kick out of it. We were doing all right. It was getting dark by then, so we started off. A whole truck-load of flares had arrived in the meantime, so it looked like we were all set.

"Yes, I'd say that happened just about between page 113 and page 114, because when you stop to think more than half a day is missing in your book. They couldn't have slept all that time, they were much too excited. I certainly don't see how Comrade Hein could have slept, because he was a strategic genius, as you call it, and a strategic genius is never allowed to sleep. Every time he starts nodding off, somebody comes running and asks him, What do we do now, Comrade Hein? I can't help feeling sorry for the little runt when I put myself in his shoes, because the whole thing started rolling by accident and he's got to keep on rolling whether he likes it or not, and to make matters worse, he has to roll forward. But maybe he thought it was fun, even if the idea doesn't appeal to you; we'd have to know him better. Come to think of it, there's not a word in your book about what the man was thinking, and that's really unfair to him. You just start a new chapter and write Bahrenfeld on top. Don't be offended, my boy, but that's unfair, even if there aren't any documents about it. Even if you weren't able to find out where this Hein came from, and even if he did vanish into thin air later on, he must have existed or they wouldn't have been able to take that picture of him. All I'm trying to say is that he must have had a home somewhere and an old mother or some such thing and maybe even a young wife who was expecting— same as me when I was detained in Hamburg by the strike. And nobody can find fault with him if he's thinking how lovely it would be to be sitting home at the table and his wife is just coming in with the soup. Because, even if he is a strategic genius, as you call it, he's only human. Even when a revolution's going on, nobody can help having such thoughts, and I don't see why you couldn't have mentioned them.

"But what you say right here on page 114, at the beginning of the chapter, really makes me angry. It's pure nonsense, and nobody can tell me different, even if I haven't been to the university. I'm saying this only to you, because it's nobody else's business, and besides, other people would probably find what you've written much more interesting than what really happened. But don't be offended, my boy, it's all wrong.

"You write . . . no, I'll have to look it up, I can't keep all those fancy words in my head . . . hm, here it is, listen to what the boy wrote: 'Considerable bloodshed was averted by his consummate diplomacy. His achievement in this regard cannot be overemphasized.' That's the limit. Where's the achievement? Just tell me that. What kind of an idiot would I be if I slugged it out when it could all be settled peaceably? You don't deserve a medal for that.

"But I wasn't referring to the achievement. I meant the other part of it. What was it you said again? Crazy. And consummate to boot. No, I don't go along. Take it from your old father, it's plain nonsense. I won't tell a soul, and you know how tight-lipped Mother is. But nonsense it is and remains. And I'll tell you why. You just didn't think it out. Look. The two or three hundred young scamps out there at the army post were high-school students and such, all wet behind the ears; they weren't soldiers. Diplomacy is all right with old soldiers, they have a feel for these things. They know when it's hopeless to go on fighting and they'd better stop. But youngsters like that want to be heroes, and that's dangerous. They've been taught how to fire a gun and throw hand grenades at the landscape, it's not hard to learn. So they don't stop to listen; all they want is to shoot and get shot, so your school books will say, 'To the last man!' and more such impractical drivel. With heroes your consummate diplomacy won't work, make a note of that for the future, because some things never change. If ever you try it, you'll only be putting your foot in it, and, consummate or not, you'll be dead before you can count three. With heroes you've got to think of something else if you don't want to shoot it out. You've got to make them so nervous they start whimpering for Mama. Well, in Bahrenfeld we made them nervous. They were so scared you could smell it for miles around.

"If there was any need of diplomacy, it was with Hundewatt. Funny the way I've gotten used to that crazy name just from seeing it printed in your book. Comrade Hundewatt was a harder nut to crack; if your Hein was able to handle him, he must have been pretty consummate, as you call it; there I agree with you. To put the damper on a man like that, a human bomb-

shell that threatens to explode at any moment, to hold
him down for hours at a time, yes, you could call that
an achievement. Especially when it all looked so simple,
with the army post surrounded by thousands of comrades, at least ten times as many as the youngsters
inside. What were we waiting for? Hundewatt was of the
kind that lower their horns and rush right in with a
let's go, boys, and everybody follows him. A man like
that can disrupt a whole army. And since the machine
gun was invented, that kind of enthusiasm doesn't get
you anywhere; holes in your belly is what it gets you.
But try to explain that to a mad bull. You'll be lucky
if he doesn't take you for a traitor.

"Where were we? That's right, in our so-called command post, not the school building, we'd left there;
the bar on the street leading to the station, on the right,
I think, coming from the army post. I knew that bar
well from my training days. If it's still there, you really
should have published a picture of it, because it's a
historical bar, so to speak. A nice cosy place, not one of
those modern-looking joints for Sunday excursionists
with their cars. Kind of a glassed-in veranda in front.
Out back there was a beer garden with tables and
benches, and chickens pecking around in between and
shitting on the benches. You had to look sharp before
you sat down. I knew the owner and his wife from my
army days, because that's where we went for our bull
sessions when we had time off. Just the place for a
command post. We told the owner and his wife not to

worry. The family lived under the roof; the noise had woken up their two kids and they were bawling. I sent Hundewatt up to calm them down and take a look around and calm himself down too. It worked. He was happy as a lark when he came down, because the kids had stopped crying and gone to sleep. A big fellow like that is good for that kind of thing; he knows how to get along with children and they like him. Then we tackled the owner. Nobody's going to hurt you, comrade, we told him, we only need your place for a command post, we're not going to break anything. Word of honor! We'll all pay for anything you give us, just tell us what we owe, discipline is the word. There won't be any other customers coming, on account of the revolution, and you needn't worry about legal hours because we're the police, so to speak. After that, it was all nice and cosy. His wife made us coffee and good thick soup. Some of the comrades had to help her peel potatoes, my orders, they had nothing else to do. It was a regular command post, with a sentry out front and couriers with their motorcycles. We'd brought the map from the school and spread it out on the table. We'd found a red pencil there too. I'd marked and numbered all the places where the comrades were waiting with their outfits. That made it look like a real command post. If only Hundewatt hadn't been so impatient. I kept having to think up things for him to do and pleading with him, Man, why can't you just sit on your behind? The floor'll cave in if you keep running around like that.

"And then came the fireworks! You can't imagine what it was like. It went on for a couple of hours, and all courtesy of old army stocks. A thing like that doesn't happen every day, and naturally the comrades enjoyed it. A fireball shoots up in one sector, and just as it's going out, they send up another somewhere else, red ones and white ones, whatever they lay their hands on. There were even a few green ones. One after another, from all directions, all around the army post. And on top of that the noise! The men with rifles fired them up in the air; they had permission. In a revolution you've got to have noise to make people believe it; otherwise they fall asleep. Upstairs in the attic window we have an observer. If the flares stop in some sector we send out a courier. What's wrong, comrades? Taking a nap? If you've run out of rockets, say the word. Oh yes, I forgot the motorcycles. The boys opened their cutouts and the noise was something terrible. We even had trucks driving around, lights out of course; with the festive illumination they didn't need any. But only in places where they couldn't be shot at from the army post. Here and there, where it wouldn't do any damage, the boys were allowed to toss a hand grenade, all for the noise. We made it sound as if a whole army corps was moving in. A hullabaloo like that can make you pretty nervous, especially at night when you can't see what's actually going on.

"That was just what we wanted. It was going off fine. The only one who wasn't satisfied was Comrade

114

Hundewatt. Every few minutes he'd bang his fist down on the table like a sledgehammer. What are we waiting for? This is treason! You just stop shooting your mouth off about treason and knocking the cups off the table, they belong to the proprietor. And don't louse up the map, we need it. Poor Comrade Hein! It's no joke holding down a wild man like that.

"After a while he sees it's no use, so the next time Hundewatt starts boiling over, he says, All right, now we'll take action. What we need is two smart girls.— Girls? Hundewatt howls. What are you going to do with girls?—Let me worry about that, comrade. Get me the owner and his wife, they'll know where to find a couple of smart girls.

"Hundewatt thinks I've gone crazy, or maybe he thinks I want the girls for myself. He gives me a funny look, but he gets the owner and his wife all the same, and just as I'd thought, the wife had an idea. How about Alma? she asks her husband. No, he says, too fat. No harm in that, I say, some like them fat, it makes them look motherly. The main thing is a head on her shoulders. So we settle for Alma. The other one's name was Wilhelmine, I think, how can I keep all these names in my head? The other one wasn't fat, but to make up for it she had a quick tongue. We send the owner's wife for the girls, we think they'll trust her more than they would us, and we send two comrades along to protect her on the street, because you never know what will happen when everybody's so excited.

The girls live right around the corner; that's where they've got their rooms and their beds. We tell her to ask if they'd care to help the revolution, seeing there couldn't be any business on a night like that. The girls are willing, they slip on their dresses and pretty up, and the bar owner's wife brings them back to our command post.

"Come to think of it, that's another place where your book isn't fair: not even mentioning those two girls."

"What girls?" I asked him.

"Alma, that was the fat one, and the other one, whatever her name was. Of course they wouldn't want their names to appear, that's understandable, but you really should have mentioned them. Because they were the ones that took Bahrenfeld, not Comrade Hein or Comrade Hundewatt either. Without those girls it wouldn't have gone off so smoothly, take it from me. By right that tablet should have been dedicated to them: TO THE UNKNOWN HEROINES."

Wasn't that clever of him? Precisely! He'd said all that so matter-of-factly. What a man my father was! Naturally I thought the two girls were an invention, all the more so as my mother couldn't refrain from saying, "Some sluts they must have been."

"No, Mother, you mustn't say that, they weren't sluts at all. Alma really was quite an imposing figure. In Uelzen it wouldn't have been possible, because everybody knows everybody else, but you can be dead sure that they've been nicely settled in life for years, with a candy store or a milk bar, and husbands and children. That's how it is in a big city.

"Well, according to your son, Comrade Hein was in the field artillery. In that case he must have known what it's like outside an army post. There's always a few fancy ladies flitting around, mostly in pairs. They waggle their rear ends as they pass the entrance. Lord, many's the time I stood guard there till my legs were coming out of my shoulders. Naturally they stop to kid us. Hi, cutie, when'll you have a little time for me? That kind of thing. We weren't allowed to answer them, that would put you in the guardhouse, but nobody could tell us not to listen or prevent us from winking at them."

"We have no difficulty in imagining that you winked at them," says my mother.

"That may be, Mother. Come to think of it, why not? All day long those boys on the post were chased around and shouted at; they were grateful for a friendly word, and something a little softer to the touch than a rifle butt wouldn't have hurt them either. That's the way it goes, the girls know it, and that's why they come around—you can't blame them. But you needn't worry about me, Mother. I wasn't exactly an angel, but all the money I had was my pay, and when you go with those girls, you've got to give them something, only death is free as they say, and they've got to live too. I got food packages from home, fine Uelzen sausages; out here in the country there was more to eat than in a city like Hamburg and Father had good connections. But he was stingy about money, he thought my pay was enough. Well, it may have been enough for a beer now and then, but not for a girl, begging your pardon. All the same, though, I kept my eyes open, it can't hurt you, and so did Comrade Hein. He must have known what was what or he wouldn't have hit on the idea with the girls. Hundewatt would never have thought of it.

"Hundewatt, the blockhead, thought they'd shoot at the girls. He said it was disgraceful to expose girls to danger when we men could handle it all much better.

"'Don't let it worry you,' I said. 'I guarantee they won't shoot at any girls. They're heroes and heroes aren't allowed to shoot at girls. They're fresh from their mothers' breasts, they'd drop their gun if they tried to shoot at a girl.' I think Hundewatt got the idea, he was a softhearted soul.

"So the two of them report to our command post. Naturally I stand up and so does Hundewatt. He even bows, he's all flustered, and I say to the landlord, 'Kindly serve the ladies something to drink, maybe a liqueur. Or would you prefer something hot?'"

"Some ladies," says my mother, turning up her nose.

"Now really, Mother, what else am I to call them? I've got to be polite, I want something of them. Of course I look them over, and right away I think, Just what we need. These little girls will stop at nothing. Comrade Hein makes a little speech. At least he tries to.

He clears his throat and starts in, 'Well, ladies, Comrade Hundewatt here and yours truly are mighty grateful to you for your willingness to help the revolution. We'll tell the rest of the comrades and they'll never forget it.' But that's as far as I get, because the little one, the one with the sharp tongue, interrupts me. 'Save your spit, kid. We don't need a sermon.' The fat one grins and says, 'Never mind calling us ladies, we're just a couple of the boys.' That was fine with me. 'The sermon,' I said, 'was only because I'm kind of shy with ladies.' The fat one grins again and says, 'You look it.' So I go on, 'And now because you're such fine girls we can get right down to the business part of it. As I've explained to the hefty comrade here, business is business, and we're all going to take up a collection so your evening won't be wasted.' Man alive, you should have seen them, like they'd been stung by a wasp. The little one jumps up, I think she's going to scratch my eyes out. 'Come on, Alma. If they're going to insult us, they can make their shitty revolution all by themselves. I'm pulling out.' But the fat one only laughs again and pulls the little one back into her chair by her skirt. 'There's a general strike on,' she says. 'That gives us a little free time, so for once we can do something for nothing.' Splendid girls, don't get angry, Mother. Comrade Hundewatt is enthusiastic too, he's waving his arms, looks like he wants to hug them for their solidarity with the toiling masses. I could see right off that the girls took a shine to Hundewatt, but he

119

couldn't talk as well as Comrade Hein, so I had to manage it all. And even if they were splendid girls, you had to watch your step with them, because you never know how they'll take a proposition like this. Before you know it, they've got the wrong idea and all your trouble is for nothing.

"Well, I says to myself, sooner started sooner finished. 'All right, girls. You know the main gate of the army post?' That was another mistake. The girls thought I was stupid. The little one doesn't even answer, and the fat one says, 'Hell, that's our territory.' Then the little one bubbled over; she had a story and she couldn't keep it in. 'I was just there,' she says. 'Thought I'd have a look. All the excitement and you've lit everything up so pretty. Your boys didn't want to let me through. I told them where to get off and to kindly mind their own business. Alma, you should have come, you've got all year to mend your bra. And who do you think was on guard? The kid that calls himself Peter; maybe that's really his name. The good-looking blond I went with a couple of times, kind of goofy, but he has money. He's standing there with a load of hand grenades in his belt, and so help me I felt sorry for him. I pass him real close and I say, Don't let those things scrape your belly off, kid. And he says, Beat it, kid, nothing doing tonight. I wouldn't think so, I say, it's much too light. I see some of the others running around in the yard right behind the gate. They've got a machine gun pointing through the bars for your special benefit.

Isn't that nice of them? One of them sticks his nose out and says, What's the trouble out here? No trouble but me, honey bunch, I tell him. Beat it, he says. Sticky weather tonight. Not so sticky, I tell him. Just cool. It's a lot warmer in my room, but if you'd rather catch pneumonia . . . and then I walk off.'

"That was good news. Exactly what I'd expected, the machine gun and their not firing on girls. The little one with her lip would start things off, then Alma would talk some sense into the youngsters, and everything would come out all right. Alma was getting impatient. 'Speak up, boys, don't be bashful. I've got my undies soaking at home. What else can a woman do with all this uproar you're making? Exactly what do you want of us?'

"I put it to her straight: 'Would you be willing to go out there again, same as usual?'

"They look at each other, they're not so sure, because they've got to be careful in their profession. Finally, the fat one, who had good practical sense, asks, 'What good will that do your revolution?'

"At that point Hundewatt almost messed everything up. He bangs his fist on the table—bam, it almost upsets the ladies' cups—and yells, 'No! It would be an eternal disgrace!'

"Then the little one blows up. 'What are you gassing about? What would be a disgrace?'

"'We can't expose our lady comrades to such a danger,' he bellows. 'Maybe those bums'll shoot.'

"That makes Alma laugh. She's in stitches. 'Don't let that worry you, big boy. Maybe they'd shoot at you, you'd be easy to hit, but at us . . .' She turns to her friend. 'What do you think?'

"'Those boys are so lovesick they'd be more likely to shoot each other,' says the little one.

"That settled it. But it wasn't easy with the ladies. One wrong word and they fly at you.

"I start in again: 'You see, we want to take that army post.' 'Do you think we're blind?' the little one cuts in. 'What else would the fireworks be for?'

"'We don't give a damn about the post itself,' I explain, 'or about the kids in there; we could starve them out if we had to. But we need their arms and vehicles, and we need them quick, because the comrades in Magdeburg have asked us to help them, and without arms we can't do it. Understand?'

"'You want us to lug them out to you?' the little one asks.

"'Of course not, you'd only sprain your beauty and get your nice dresses dirty. Now listen seriously like two sensible girls. It wouldn't be hard to take the post. We've got it surrounded and we've got plenty of comrades just waiting to barge in. We could do it, and we wouldn't need any girls. But those kids in there want to be heroes, they'd fight back. That doesn't scare us. A few people might get killed, but that's how it is in a revolution.—You pipe down, Comrade Hundewatt, when I'm explaining to the ladies. You don't have to show them what a big brave man you are, they can tell by looking at you.—But there's something else to consider, and that's why I'm talking to you girls. If we storm the post like the big man says and a few comrades are shot dead, the other comrades will get mad— we men are stupid that way. There'll be a blood bath and all those young pipsqueaks will be killed. That would be too bad.—No, comrade, you keep quiet, the ladies understand this better than you. That would really be a disgrace to the revolution. Why hadn't we reasoned with them? That's what everybody would want to know. And that's why we've got to work out a better idea with the ladies.'

"Alma, the fat one, agrees. She says it would be a damn shame, and maybe those kids would still grow up to be decent people. 'But what can two girls do about it?' asks the perky little one.

"At least they were ready to hear my plan.

"'Take a look at this map,' I said. 'We swiped it from the school in Altona.'

"The girls weren't especially interested. They knew the neighbourhood without a map.

"'All right. Here where I'm putting my finger is the army post. And here's this bar, only a couple of hundred yards away. We've got our men here and here and here, all around it, wherever you see the red numbers. Plenty of men and they're keeping their eyes open; they won't let anybody through.

"'Our boys are itching to attack; their feet are

123

freezing and they'd like to be moving. You can see by the fireworks that the post is surrounded, and the kids inside have noticed it too. If you ask me, they're getting very nervous, because they're trapped. Is that clear?

"'Fine. Then I'll continue. Now I'm going to show you something that nobody's noticed, not even the comrade here with his thick head. Up here on the map, that's north, up here north of the army post, a little to the right of Luruper Feld, there are no flares going up, as you'd see if you looked out the attic window.—Good grief, Jumbo's exploding again. Can't you sit still for half a second while I explain to the ladies? If you didn't notice it's because you were blinded by the fireworks. What a pest you are. Just stop interrupting, the girls want to get this over with, they need their sleep.—As I was saying, there's a kind of gap in the circle up here. None of our men are posted there, that's why there're no fireworks. Which is intentional, even if nobody noticed. Is that clear?

"'Fine. Well, my idea was that the two of you should stroll over to the gate same as usual, as if nothing were wrong, and talk to the youngsters on guard . . . They wouldn't listen to me, and they certainly wouldn't listen to Jumbo here, or we'd do it ourselves . . . and tell them about that gap in the circle. You'll have to pretend you discovered it all by yourselves and you're only telling them because you're softhearted women and they're so young and you can't help feeling sorry for them. Just be sweet and reasonable, or be any way you like, you know better than I do, you don't need any advice from me. As long as you tell them that up there to the right of Luruper Feld the road to Oldesloe is open, and if they want to be dear, good boys, they can still get away.'

"Naturally Hundewatt flared up again. He was probably going to yell treason, but this time the girls did my job for me. The little perky one laced into him, he didn't know what had hit him. 'Let the little runt finish, you blockhead, he's ten times smarter than you.' And Alma put on the finishing touches. 'You've got so much muscle there's no room for brains.'

"After that I was able to go on with my speech. 'Of course they'll think it's a trap to get them out of the building. I'd think so myself in their place. So we'll give you girls a note. Maybe you won't have to use it, that depends on the circumstances. It's entirely up to you, because you know how to talk to young heroes better than we do. What time is it now? Half-past twelve, high time for bed. All right, let's figure it out. It ought to be about one by the time you get to the gate and start talking. Suppose we suggest four o'clock in the morning, that ought to be time enough. That'll give them three full hours to make up their minds. Because naturally there'll be a big argument about honor and suchlike rubbish, and that'll make them more nervous than ever. But there won't be any rush, plenty of time to do up their packs and clear out. It won't be light yet, they won't be embarrassed, they'll even think they've put one over on us. That's what you've got to tell them. And if they don't trust you girls or the note either, we can arrange to give them some kind of signal once we know they've made up their minds. For instance, we could stop the flares and sound effects fifteen minutes before they're supposed to move out, then they won't feel so exposed. What do you think, comrade, would it be possible to send the motorcycle boys around to the outposts quickly enough?'

"'Sure, it's possible,' Hundewatt grumbles. 'I could go myself, but I don't understand . . .'

"'Let me worry about that, you'll understand soon enough. We need those arms and we need them quickly if we're going to help the comrades in Magdeburg. It doesn't matter a bit whether you understand or not, the ladies have caught on long ago. The main thing is for the young heroes to trust the girls.'

"'What about the note?' asks the little perky one.

"'You'll get your note. All the time I've been talking I've been drafting it in my noodle. But it's not so simple. How do they know where a note comes from or whether what it says is true? We haven't got the right kind of a stamp to make it look official, and that's too bad, because how can we expect them to trust you girls without a stamp? It's a problem. Suppose I put myself in their shoes, standing on guard, jittery from all the flares and sound effects. You girls come along with your story about Oldesloe and so on, and you've got this note. I don't know as I'd trust you . . .'

"'Never mind about that,' says Alma with her special kind of laugh. 'Leave it to us.' And of course the little one has to put in her two-cents' worth. 'We could even wrap up a wise guy like you,' she says.

"'That may be,' I say. 'Let's try it after we've got this revolution licked; that'll be our reward for all the excitement. But now we're in a hurry so I'd better mark out the road to Luruper Feld.'

"'What for?' the little one snaps. 'Do you think we're from Stupidville?'

"'Not at all, but there're a few ticklish places where you could get into trouble, and that's what we want to avoid. Because naturally those boys will have to leave their weapons behind, and they won't like that. For all I care they can stuff a pistol or two in their pockets, but they've got to leave the machine guns and the artillery if there is any, and especially the vehicles, or we guarantee nothing. Because naturally we'll notice it if they take too much stuff, and then the deal is off. And when they get to Oldesloe, they'd better scatter and keep on going, to Mecklenburg if they like. Their landowner friends will hide them in the haylofts, and they can wait for things to blow over. Maybe you could promise to be faithful to them in the meantime, that sounds nice, or anything a girl might say on such an occasion. Don't laugh, Comrade Alma, an old soldier like me knows how it is and how those boys feel. Anything to sweeten the pill. Or maybe you could tell them it's no disgrace, far from it; in fact, it's their patriotic duty to save

127

their skins, because the fatherland may need them some-day.'

"When he heard that, Hundewatt was so mad he upset his chair. I had to come down on him hard. 'Aren't you ashamed of yourself, comrade? We all know that fatherland is an old-fashioned word, but it's the kind of word that appeals to heroes. It seems to me I've heard something about the workers' fatherland, and if you haven't, you're some comrade. So don't fly off the handle and make an ass of yourself in front of the ladies. Now, we've wasted enough time. Let's draft this note.'

"But then the little one, who had a head on her shoulder, almost punctured the whole idea. She brought up an objection that pretty near floored even me. 'How can we be sure the whole thing isn't a put-up job? Once we've persuaded them to beat it unarmed, what's to prevent you from shooting them down? What would that make us look like?'

"There I was stymied; I could see the girls didn't really trust me. But at that point Hundewatt showed what he was good for. He saved the situation. He puffed up to twice his size with dignity and started bumbling: something about honor, revolutionary morality, personal responsibility, and so on. The phrases just poured out of him. He even said something about discipline, though that didn't go over too well with the ladies. Luckily Alma started laughing or he'd have gone on forever. When she'd finished laughing, she said to the little one, 'Jumbo really means it, just look at him.

All right, give us your note, or we'll never get to bed, and tomorrow we'll have crow's feet.'

"So you see, my son, a revolution isn't as simple as it says in your book. Any fool can storm an army post but getting all those muddleheads to stick to a plan took some doing, you've got to give your Comrade Hein credit. Even I'm surprised that he didn't let the whole thing go hang.

"This note now. I guess it hasn't been preserved or you'd have mentioned it in your book. It certainly existed, you can take your old father's word for it, but I suppose the youngsters threw it away or burned it when they'd gotten away safely and they didn't need it any more. Obviously they wouldn't have wanted a historical document about their evacuation laying around, because even if it was good sense, there wasn't much glory in it. Well, we had quite a time with that note.

"'Let's get started,' I said. 'Serve the ladies some more coffee, comrade bartender, or they'll catch cold on us. And get me a sheet of writing paper, anyway some kind of paper. It doesn't have to be anything special, just tear a sheet out of your ledger; in a revolution you don't have to write your love letters on monogrammed stationery. All right. Now I'll put it down in my best handwriting, and you can all sing out if there's anything you don't like. Here goes:

The undersigned, charged by the Provisional Government . . .

129

"'Is that the right name for it?' I ask Hundewatt. Provisional Government was all right with him, though we had no idea whether any such thing existed.

The undersigned, charged by the Provisional Government with the conduct of military affairs, pledge themselves . . .

"'No, that's no good. We can't say military because we're anti-militarists. There's another word, something beginning with ex, I've read it somewhere. Ex . . . ex . . . damn it, no, not examination or example. Ex . . . ex . . . I've got it! Executive. Glory be, that's the right word in a revolution, that'll put their eye out.

The executive committee of the Provisional Government pledge themselves by their revolutionary honor . . .'

"Revolutionary honor was for Hundewatt's sake. He nodded his thick head. That appealed to him.

. . . pledge themselves by their revolutionary honor to grant the garrison of the Bahrenfeld army post unmolested passage at any time up to 4 a.m. over the roads leading northward in the direction of Oldesloe.'

"As I explain to Hundewatt and the ladies, this is intentional. It seems better just to give the direction and not to specify any particular highway, because maybe the youngsters would rather sneak off on back roads, and that would suit us too.

On the sole condition that all heavy weapons and ammunition must be left in good condition at the army post.

"'Rifles too,' Hundewatt puts in. But I say, No,

130

comrade. I'm not mentioning rifles, I leave that to the girls. Tell them that rifles would only make them look suspicious, they can't hide a rifle in their trouser pocket. Something on that order. We proceed:

The army post is under constant observation . . .'

"'Well, with the fireworks they've probably noticed that all by themselves.

. . . Removal of said objects would be noticed without delay, whereupon the undersigned would regard their pledge as null and void.

"Doesn't that sound like a lawyer? Now all we need is a last sentence, and we want that to sound like something a pastor would say at confirmation exercises.

If contrary to our expectation the post has not been evacuated by 4 a.m., the revolution will wash its hands in innocence.

"'No, that's no good. There's got to be something about blood.

. . . the blood that is shed will for all time . . . yes, for all time *. . . remain a blemish . . .* yes, a blemish *. . . from which the enemies of progress will never be able to wash themselves clean.*

"'Or how about a bloody blemish?

"'Then all we need is:

Given at Bahrenfeld Headquarters. . . .

"'. . . and the date. Headquarters will make an impression, I can promise you that, especially if you girls give them a song and dance about the activity here.

"'Well, what do you say, Comrade Hundewatt? Do we affix our Friedrich Wilhelm?'

"Believe it or not, this dumbbell wanted us to put in Heil Moscow at the bottom. I felt like climbing up the wall. And the girls were ripping mad because they were tired and wanted to go to bed sometime.

"'You've got to be diplomatic,' I told him. 'Your Heil Moscow will only get their dander up. It's waving a red flag in their faces. And think of the girls. Do you want them to go marching in with a Heil Moscow and their fists in the air? They've got better things to do with their hands. We'll have plenty of time for Heil Moscows when it's all over.'

"Well, he finally calms down and we sign the note: Hundewatt and Hein. Alma, the fat one, puts it in her big pocketbook, the kind those girls always go around with.

"'That does it,' I say. I stand up very solemnly. 'It remains only for Comrade Hundewatt and me— stand up, comrade—to thank you ladies for your sacrifice to the revolution. The revolution will never forget it. Here and now in the name of the people we wish to assure you . . .'

"I didn't get any further. The little one interrupts with one word: 'Applesauce.' Alma laughs. 'Never mind the soapboxing. It's too late at night.'

"'Suits me,' I say. 'But just one more thing to set the seal on our happy understanding. How about giving Comrade Hundewatt a little kiss? He's all hot and bothered, he needs it bad.'

"Alma is only too glad, she puts her heart in it. Hundewatt goes red in the face, because he doesn't know if it's compatible with party discipline. And the little perky one? Well, she looks up at me and says, 'What about you, kid? Don't you need one?'

"'Maybe I do,' I say. 'Let's talk it over when things quieten down.'

"Don't glare, Mother, you've got to play along with the girls to keep them in a good humor. Then the ladies leave, and I can't believe my eyes. Naturally we escort them out; Hundewatt has to give the comrades instruction to let them through and keep a discreet eye on them in case they need help. And so help me, I can't believe my eyes. Damned if the little one doesn't see fit to waggle her rear end."

That was too much for my mother. She couldn't contain herself. "Well, Father," she says, "as I know you and your eyes, I'd say you believed them all right." And then we had another good laugh at my father's expense.

"Well, maybe I did. If I'd seen it on Lüneburger Strasse here in Uelzen, I'd tend to believe my old eyes. But then, with all the excitement and shooting, I couldn't get over it. Revolution or not, she waggles her sweet little rear end. At a time when everybody was thinking of the revolution, same as tonight we're all thinking of this book your boy has written, because if he hadn't written it we wouldn't know one thing about the whole story—it happened so long ago.

"You've got the rest of it perfectly right, I can't see any objection, the way our plan worked and the youngsters moved out, and about the arms we found, but not as much as we'd expected. And you were right about that old armored car that was sitting in the yard all ready for us. Good old Hundewatt was out of his mind; he climbed up on top and shouted Heil Moscow. Except for the death's head the young heroes had daubed on it with chalk or white paint. You could have mentioned that."

"But Father," I asked him, "how do you know all that?"

"My goodness, how do I know? You've thought up a hard one, haven't you? Well, I'm only an old Heath peasant, and here's how I look at it. It's like theory and practice, as you call it. You've got your science, you've collected these documents, so you can explain the significance of it all even if you weren't there, because you weren't born until several months later. Which is very impressive, and so is the hard work you put into it. But a practical old codger like me can't help scratching his head and wondering—don't be offended now—what really happened when all these people were in the thick of it with their hands full and no time to think about documents or significance. That's why I concentrated on the two girls."

"Father, I'm not referring to these girls you've conjured up. Even if they had really existed, the course of historical events would be pretty much the same. No,

I'm referring to the death's head on the armored car."

"That just shows you weren't alive yet, or you'd know those right-wing youngsters always did that. It wouldn't even have scared a little girl, and an old soldier like Comrade Hein could only shake his head at their childishness. If we had a photograph of that armored car, you'd see that I'm right. But it probably wasn't light enough in the yard that morning to take a picture, or maybe the gentlemen of the press were catching up on their sleep.—But now that the army post has finally been taken and your book has been published, let's stop working ourselves up over ancient history. Too much of it is boring and your mother's getting cranky."

I could have let well enough alone, my father was offering me an honorable peace. But I couldn't let go. I suppose I felt that my father covered me and my book with ridicule, and in trying to extricate myself I just got in deeper and deeper. Beg your pardon? Like a Baron Münchhausen in reverse? Precisely. A perfect metaphor, thank you. And now maybe you can tell me how I'm going to extricate myself from my own sense of ridicule?

Because how can we be sure that it was my father's intention to ridicule me? Actually I doubt it, and that makes me unhappy. Yes, he sometimes made fun of academicians, it was a kind of habit with him. Still, in this case there must have been some other reason for what he did. But what reason? Precisely because I think I know him and because, forgive the pathos, I cherish his memory, I don't believe he wanted to demolish my book. He would hardly have done that in the presence of my mother and my fiancée. If at all, he'd have done it in private. But what then was the purpose of such a performance at our engagement celebration? What was his motive? He could just as well have kept silent about his old experiences. As far as I know, he'd never spoken of them before and never did afterwards, neither to my mother nor anyone else, certainly not to his friends. Friends! I wonder if he had any. He was well liked in Uelzen and he was always glad to help people. But friends? I can't conceive of his having a friend he would have confided in. Who has friends? you say. Right again. A man has a wife and children and colleagues and cronies, but when we speak of friends, it's romantic sentimentality.

What did my father have in mind? Why did he have to play the clown, as my mother called it, that evening? It wasn't to boast of his youthful follies. If he'd wanted to do that, he could have spoken openly. And he had no need to justify himself, because nobody knew a thing about all this. Is that why he cried in the hospital? Did he cry over his two weeks of revolution and over Comrade Hundewatt, whom they killed in 1933 in the Hohe Bleichen? Did he cry because he was so alone, because in his position as a successful businessman he had no one he could talk to about it, not even his son?

136

Obviously he couldn't unburden himself to the two women at his bedside. I can't help having these thoughts. Yes, of course. You're right, it can happen to anyone. That's why it's good to have relatives present; then you can say, Don't get excited, it's all for the best. Or even a clergyman, because you wouldn't want to disappoint him. But this happens to be my father, and that's why I get these ideas. Do you know what? If I'd known in time, I'd have had him dressed in his old suit, the one with the Rathenow label, even if it was a size too big for him, to make him feel happy in his coffin at least. It may sound sentimental, I don't care.

Forgive the digression. We'll have to be going soon, and you'd like to know what happened next that evening. As I've told you, nothing would have happened, my father had no further desire to talk about the book. But I had to puff myself up, on account of my fiancée, I suppose. I must have wanted her to admire my knowledge of history, or some such thing. Yes, perfectly ridiculous, and how my father must have laughed to himself at my conceit.

I complimented him again for the vividness of his narration. I even admitted that it could all have happened as he said, though it wouldn't have altered the historical facts in any way. Yes, I complimented him. I thought I was making a shrewd move that would make my father back down. As if you could flatter an old Heath peasant into doing anything against his will! It only makes him suspicious.

137

"Even if we assume that everything happened as you say in Hamburg and Bahrenfeld," I argued, "we must bear in mind that the victory in Hamburg was only a successful preparation for the subsequent events. History would speak at most of an insignificant local insurrection if this beginning had not been followed by the admirable diversionary maneuver, the march on Magdeburg. That was what actually turned the tide in favor of the revolutionaries and, what's more, without any appreciable bloodshed."

My father didn't want to go into it. "You've dealt with that very thoroughly in your book, there's no need to say any more about it. Think of it, Mother, the boy has written more than two hundred pages, with documents and photographs to be sure of getting it right. And the whole business only lasted nine or ten days. It's hard to believe that anybody could write two hundred pages about it. No, my boy, there's nothing to add. It's simply amazing what you've done with those few days."

"That's not the point, Father."

"Yes, it is. The most you could say is that it's too bad the Nazis killed Hundewatt, because the poor fellow could have told you a good deal; for instance, how he organized all that and in such a hurry. There aren't many men who could do that. Getting the freight cars to transport the men and equipment. And the comrades had to be fed during those ten days. Really, that almost makes him a genius, as you call it. To judge by his picture and your description, he must have had amazing energy, not to mention his enthusiasm for his revolution. And what luck, Mother, that they didn't march to Magdeburg via Uelzen, which would have been the shortest route; we'd have had the revolution in our peaceful old town, with you expecting and all."

"It's all stuff and nonsense," said my mother.

"Don't say that, Mother. If it was all stuff and nonsense, your boy wouldn't have written a book about it."

"You're only putting it on, Father."

"What do you mean, putting it on?"

"You're only playing dumb. You know perfectly well what I'm talking about and what my whole book is about: the genius of the man, pretending to march on Magdeburg, suddenly turning off at Wittenberge, passing Magdeburg by and advancing on Berlin in forced marches."

"Where's the genius in that?"

"Please don't interrupt. I believe my book proves conclusively that this stratagem originated with Comrade Hein and moreover that it went counter to the intentions of the party leadership. Their plan was that we should help defend Magdeburg against the Bavarian free corps. Neither in Hamburg nor in Berlin was the urgency of this plan doubted. At first Comrade Hein seems to have subscribed to it. In any case, he let it be known that he was taking the revolutionary troops, as we may as well call them, to Magdeburg. Here in the appendix I have a facsimile of a leaflet printed, as the date shows, after the Bahrenfeld army post was taken. Pure luck, incidentally, that the document has come down to us. It was kept by a private collector, who left his archive to the public library. This leaflet calls on the population to help the people of Magdeburg and to give the troops from Hamburg all possible support. Of course it's written in the jargon of the time, the German is rather primitive, but that doesn't alter the fact that the original destination was Magdeburg. Why they didn't go by way of Uelzen and Stendal can no longer be determined. Maybe the road was blocked, but that's not the essential, Father. The essential is the feint, which completely fooled the leaders of the free corps. And that's my central theme: how could a man of the people, whom no one had ever heard of, a nobody thrown to the surface by the revolution, so to speak, have turned out to be such a tactical genius? You're free to make fun of my limited historical perspective, but the phenomenon must be of interest to you, and that's why I'm asking you."

"You don't have to be a genius for that," my father grumbled. He seemed to have lost all interest in the conversation. "Any child in Uelzen would have done exactly what your Comrade Hein did, unless he was feebleminded."

"I don't catch your meaning."

"There you have it, Mother. It's just like I've always said. With all the education they funnel into them at the university, these young people don't seem to know the simplest things any more. They're too impractical to change their own diapers. Look here, my boy, when I want something I don't point my finger at it, that would be stupid. Suppose you want to buy a cow. The farmer takes you into his barn. You take a shine to one of them, she looks like the best of the lot. What do you do? Maybe in passing you give her a little pat on the rump, no more, but then you step up to another that's not so good. How much is this one? you ask. Naturally the farmer thinks, Here's a man I can cheat. He states a price, it's much too high; you tell him what you're inclined to pay, much too little of course. Then the haggling starts. You keep it up for half an hour or so; then you say, No, I'm afraid that's more than I can afford, and you make for the door as if the deal were off. At the door you stop, you put on that you're sorry and take a last look around. Then finally you point at the cow you wanted in the first place and ask kind of offhand-like, How much do you want for this one here? By that time the bargaining has broken the farmer down and he's discouraged because the deal has fallen through. That way you get your cow a good deal cheaper than he ever intended. Well, that's how business is done, every child knows that, and your Comrade Hein knew it too if he had any sense."

"What has that got to do with Hein?"

"How can you be so dense? You've told us all about it yourself in two hundred pages. If I understand it, it must be perfectly clear to you as a scholar. Those free-corps people from Bavaria made one mistake. They underestimated the other fellow's intelligence, and that's always a mistake. It's the same as with the cow, you don't point at the one you want. Comrade Hein must have caught on right away. They're trying to pull the wool over our eyes, that's what he said to himself. What would those fellows from Bavaria want with Magdeburg? That's eyewash and it doesn't take me in. Because military affairs, or whatever you want to call them, are no different from business; you don't tell the world what you're after. What did those fellows from Bavaria want with Magdeburg? There's plenty of industry in Magdeburg, but the Bavarians wouldn't march north for industry. They'd march north for political reasons or whatever you want to call them. Magdeburg is only a second-rate cow; what they really want to buy is Berlin, it's plain as day. Don't forget that those free-corps men were old soldiers. All right. We know their game, but when you know the enemy's game, you've got to pretend not to, any child knows that. My guess is that your Comrade Hein said to himself, All right, we'll print a leaflet to make them think we've fallen for their Magdeburg dodge. Besides, he probably thought it would please his comrades in Hamburg who didn't know the score. And I wouldn't let the funny German bother me. It's the kind of German the comrades understood. He wasn't writing a school essay. Anyway, it worked. You've got it all in your book and I don't see why we should waste any more words on it."

"But why did they turn off precisely at Wittenberge?"

"You mustn't ask me that, son. It's a long time since I studied geography. But look at the map here in your book. The Elbe makes a sharp bend at Wittenberge. I don't pretend to be a genius, but if you're going to Berlin, I'd call it a waste of time to follow the bend. In the meantime, it must have dawned on the comrades in Berlin that the troops from Bavaria, the whites, as they were called at the time, weren't heading for Magdeburg but were making straight for Berlin. You see, the whites weren't having such an easy time of it either, what with the strike and the unfriendly population. Most people were too scared to do much, but nobody wanted the Kaiser back. So the free corps couldn't get ahead very fast, which was lucky for us. It gave your Comrade Hein time to send the Berlin comrades a telegram from Wittenberge—you've printed it—telling them to hightail it out of Berlin and join us somewhere in between so as to catch the whites in pincers. If you take a good look at the map, Wittenberge was about the last place to turn off. Well, that's exactly what happened. As I've already told you, those free-corps men were no greenhorns, they were old front-line soldiers. It didn't take them long to realize that, if they blundered into the pincers, they'd all be killed. So they disbanded and slipped away to Mecklenburg, it was easy with all those lakes. Some of them gave themselves up in Güstrow and let themselves be disarmed. Then they went quietly home and nobody bothered them. They became Nazis later, which is a damn shame, I agree, but there was no way of knowing that at the time, you can't blame the comrades. No, what you say in your two hundred pages is all right, I can't see a thing to find fault with."

Then my mother's patience snapped. She refused to hear one more word about my book. My father thought she was right. But some devil had got into me.

"Please, Mother, forgive me. Just one more little question."

"What has all this stuff and nonsense got to do with your father?" She was really indignant.

"Nothing, Mother. I know that, but please bear with me, I know you'll understand. He wasn't directly involved, so of course he can't be expected to supply me with historical facts that may have escaped me. But he was alive and what's more he was in Hamburg at the time. Quite aside from the historical facts, I'm interested in the atmosphere of those days. And about that Father knows more than anyone else."

"I can't bear it," says my mother. "You and your atmosphere. Why don't you ask me what it was like here in Uelzen? We were miserable. That strike! Nothing worked. Even the lights went out. By sheer luck Grandfather had kept a barrel of kerosene in the cellar. I remember well. And to cap the climax, your father here was ten days late in getting home."

"Twelve days, Mother," my father corrected her. "Let's not forget the historical truth."

"Twelve days then, that makes it even worse. And if those lazy tramps hadn't finally stopped their strike, he'd still be roaming around Hamburg today, sending us a postcard now and then. That's the historical truth."

"There you have it," said my father. "The pinch of salt is still furious with me for not sending enough picture postcards. If we go on talking about your book any longer, it will turn out that I was to blame for the whole business."

I've quoted that verbatim, mind you. I haven't made anything up. Beg your pardon? An out-and-out confession? Precisely. Except that you weren't there and you didn't join in the laughter when my father made his so-called confession, in the process of poking good-natured fun at my mother. That's why, at the risk of boring you, I've been telling you all the incidentals of that evening. I myself know that I somehow betrayed my father. Maybe that sounds too dramatic. Betrayed him to whom? you might ask. Maybe my father wanted to be betrayed. But let's not go into that.

Now pay attention. Because then he spoke even more plainly, so plainly that today I can only regard it as a moral slap in the face.

"Even if we assume," I said to my father, "that

everything happened as you suppose, without benefit of genius so to speak, we're still faced with a riddle: why, at the height of his triumph, did Comrade Hein suddenly vanish from the face of the earth? No, Father, wait. His disappearance is and remains a historical fact. No wonder legends sprang up. I ask you: why does a man disappear, especially at the moment of victory? Or, since in criticizing my book you've chosen to put yourself in Comrade Hein's shoes, let's put it this way: if you had been Comrade Hein, what would have led you to sneak away?"

You might say that my question was as pointed as my father's confession. Except that I asked it in abysmal ignorance, and my father knew it. He scratched his head.

"To answer that, my boy, we'd have to know your Hein a good deal better. The two photographs aren't enough to know something about his life."

"Nothing whatever is known about his life."

"There. You see? Maybe he didn't want anything to be known. Such things happen."

"No, Father, wait. You don't seem to understand my question."

"No, I must be too stupid."

"According to the legend, he was murdered by the reactionaries. It's plausible, plenty of murders were being committed by right-wing extremists. That legend was the product of his baffling disappearance. It may or may not be true; we have no proof either way. The famous telegram from Uelzen is anything but proof. AM WELL. DON'T WORRY. BEST OF LUCK. YOUR COMRADE HEIN. It hardly suits the situation."

"He sounds like a joker to me."

"Precisely! And we have no proof whatever that this joker was identical with Comrade Hein. But what I was getting at is this. After careful critical study of the documents relating to Comrade Hein's activities during those twelve days, I have a strong feeling—yes, Father, only a feeling, it carries no scientific weight—that he wasn't murdered. It simply doesn't fit in with our—admittedly meager—testimony about him."

"I agree with you there. I was glad to read that in your book. The man was too smart to let himself be trapped and murdered by those rascals. You said that very nicely."

"Splendid. That gives us at least one point of agreement. But in that case, can you suggest one credible motive for his vanishing from the face of the earth?"

"A motive?"

"Yes. Or a reason?"

"Vanishing from the face of the earth?"

"Please, Father. It's only a silly metaphor. Maybe he's still alive, but that's not the point. You know perfectly well what I mean. Why did he withdraw from the movement and vanish from our historical purview?"

"Historical purview? That's a subject in itself. Maybe some people don't care for it."

"You know it's just another metaphor. Why are you always making fun of me?"

"Who's making fun of you? You mustn't keep getting angry at your old father. I only meant that if the joker is still alive, maybe he's at large here in Uelzen. Maybe he's even come into our store. Hear that, Mother? We'd better keep our eyes open. Of course, the photographs wouldn't help you—how old would he be now? About my age. But there must be some way of recognizing the rascal. Wouldn't it be a good joke if now, thirty years later, we were to corner him here in the store? I'd like to see his face if suppose he's buying Swiss cheese or Villingen stogies and Mother comes up behind him and says, Good morning, Comrade Hein, and how are you feeling this fine morning? It would be a big help to your boy here with his historical purview. Don't look so glum, my boy. Just tell me what you want of me."

"I've told you several times. It has definitely been established that after the free corps had been disbanded and the troops from Berlin and Hamburg had converged in Rathenow, Comrade Hein took part in a conference in that town. I presume it had been called to deliberate on the first steps to be taken after the victory. In the course of that conference, which must have been rather long, he disappeared and was never seen again. Can you think of a reason for this, a reason as simple as the rest of your explanations? We have at least two authentic statements by eyewitnesses. They both say the same thing: We thought he had to go to the toilet. It wasn't until an hour later that we began to be surprised at his not coming back."

"Aha," said my father and scratched his head again. "So he had to go to the toilet."

"Toilet or not is irrelevant, Father; beside the point."

"Don't be offended, my boy, but there you're making a mistake. Sometimes people get funny ideas in the toilet, I do myself. Maybe that's where he decided to bow out, it's perfectly possible. There's usually a mirror over the washbasin in those public toilets. Nobody gives it a thought, and then all of a sudden you see yourself in it; it must have given him a start to see himself. What am I doing here? he says to himself. And then he slips out the back door and goes home. But he must have had a rabbit's foot if he got away with it, because when you stop to think, it couldn't have been so easy. All right, let's drink to Comrade Hein's rabbit's foot."

"If you think the phenomenon is adequately explained by toilet and rabbit's foot, I agree that further discussion is superfluous."

"You know I've never been to the university, son. You mustn't be offended."

"I'm not offended. The historical facts speak for themselves. But to me the sudden disappearance, at the height of his triumph, of the man who at the moment was undoubtedly the leading figure in the whole campaign will always represent a human question mark, even if it's not a historical problem."

"What was the name of that old tailor, Mother, the one from Oldenstadt, the bandy-legged hunchback? We children used to call him question mark and we got our ears boxed for it."

"It couldn't have been him," said my mother. "He was killed in the first war. The name was Redbeard."

"Redbeard, that's it, and the poor man never even had a beard. I only thought of him because of the human question mark. But let's not forget that you were born a few months later, because if you hadn't been, you couldn't have written your book and you couldn't have gotten yourself engaged either. Prost!"

I was almost ready to give up. My fiancée was signaling me to stop. This was my last chance, so to speak, to avoid that moral slap in the face—now, twenty years later, I can still feel the sting of it. I meant to give up. If I didn't succeed, it was just that I had no rabbit's foot, as my father puts it. We had a little wine all around. Then, to hide my disgruntlement, I stood up and headed for the toilet, just by way of an interruption. I'm sorry to be mentioning such trifles, but if I don't you won't understand the situation. I suppose I thought they'd be talking about something else when I got back, which was just what I wanted. But I was unlucky.

I was at the door when my father called after me, "You see how it is, son, you've got to go to the toilet. But don't try to vanish from your purview; it's not so easy here in Uelzen, we'll nab you before you know it."

Maybe the thought that they'd go on laughing behind my back was more than I could bear. I could describe my feeling with greater precision, but never mind. Anyway I turned around in the doorway. And then I got personal. What presumption! As though I had a right to cross-examine my father.

I asked him a direct question. Yes, it's amazing how directly I approached the truth without suspecting it, and what a direct answer my father gave me. "Why," I asked him, "did you, in the person of Comrade Hein, leave that conference in Rathenow on the pretext of having to go to the toilet?"

"It wasn't a pretext, my boy. I really had to. You've got to take care of your bladder in a revolution."

"Then why didn't you go back to the conference afterward? Why did you take French leave?"

"They didn't need me any more."

"They didn't need you any more? What do you mean? How can you know that?"

"They had their victory; that's a historical fact, as you call it in your book. Anything else they had to discuss was their business, they knew more about it than I did, I'd have only been in the way. That's why I went to the toilet."

"You didn't consider it your moral obligation to go on helping them?"

"No, I'm sorry, I wasn't moral enough for that, and they really didn't need me any more."

151

"But the victory, Father? The fruits of victory?"

"That was their business, my boy, not mine. I was superfluous, so to speak."

"Superfluous? How could you or Comrade Hein be superfluous? How could the outstanding figure of those two weeks be superfluous?"

"It's the kind of idea you get in the toilet. But these fruits of victory. What kind of fruit is that? Mother and I sell fruit, apples and oranges in season, and canned peaches."

"I can't understand you, Father. You, Comrade Hein that is, could have played an enormous role. Every opportunity was open to you. At the very least they'd have made you mayor of Hamburg, but more likely, if you'd gone to Berlin with them, you'd have been elected to the Provisional Government. If only out of gratitude for what you'd done. Or in view of your military talents you might have been made minister of war, it's not inconceivable. Comrade Hein was no fool. He must have known all that. And now you're trying to tell me he threw away this golden opportunity for no other reason than going to the toilet. I can't accept that, Father. Nobody would."

"Hm," said my father. "That sounds like a reproach. I'm very sorry if I didn't do the right thing."

"I'm not reproaching you, that's absurd. All I want is a rational explanation."

"Would you really have wanted to be a cabinet minister's son?" my father asked.

152

That was my slap in the face and I didn't know it. He had the laughs on his side again and I laughed too. What else could I do?

But what a slap in the face! For me as his son, but also as a historian. Consider the consequences if my father had stayed with the movement and accepted a position in the government. What would have become of him in 1933, or of myself, for that matter? At best we'd have had to emigrate, but more likely my father would have been murdered like Hundewatt. Still, he couldn't have known that at the time. No, I deserved my slap in the face for regarding my father as a political careerist. What an insult!

It was all over, except that my father capitalized a little on the laughter. "What a chance we missed, Mother! Think of it. I can just see you as a Frau Minister, holding your train in one hand and a glass of champagne in the other at some reception at the ministry, surrounded by foreigners in uniform, kissing your hand and complimenting you in French and Russian. And me beside you in a Prince Albert with a big ribbon across my chest. To think that my pinch of salt could have been a Frau Minister and we missed out on it. And what has it gotten us? A self-service store. But no use crying over spilt milk. I propose a toast to the unknown hero's wife!"

"Stuff and nonsense!" said my mother. And that was the end of it.

Waiter. Bill please. No, it's the least I can do after

talking about my private affairs all evening. Even a historian gets a touch of honesty now and then.

Beg your pardon? In all the eighteen years since that engagement party did I never wonder how it had been possible for my father to relate those events in such minute detail? There you've got me by the short hair, as my father would say. No, not once. I slept the sleep of my academic superiority. It took that damned suit to wake me up. I'd rather not think about those eighteen years.

Do you know what? Strictly speaking, among ourselves, I feel like an old man compared to my father. To me he was my old man, you know how it is, a son has to have an old man. And now it turns out that he was a hundred times younger than I ever was. Beg your pardon? Yes, right you are. We come to know our fathers much too late. Precisely!

Waiter, where's that check? It's always like this when you want to pay up, they're always taking a nap. Let's get up and put our coats on. That will bring them running.